THE WOMEN'S DIRECTORY

The Voice of the Voluntary Sector
Promoting the interests and effectiveness of voluntary organisations

NCVO was established in 1919 as the representative body for charities and other organisations in England. NCVO's membership consists of 575 national members ranging from smaller self-help organisations to the biggest national charities.

NCVO has three main functions: to assist voluntary organisations through advice and information in improving their effectiveness; to promote the interests of voluntary organisations by taking part in the debate on policy issues; and to identify the need for new voluntary action in particular fields. The latter role has led NCVO to establish new organisations over the years, including Age Concern, the citizens advice bureaux network and the Charities Aid Foundation.

National Council for Voluntary Organisations
26 Bedford Square, London WC1B 3HU
Tel 071-636 4066 Fax 071-436 3188

BEDFORD SQUARE PRESS

Bedford Square Press is the publishing imprint of the National Council for Voluntary Organisations. It publishes books on a wide range of current social issues. Series published include Survival Handbooks, Community Action, Practical Guides, Directories, Reports, Organisation and Management, and Fundraising. If you would like to receive a copy of the latest Bedford Square Press catalogue, please write to:
Sales Manager
Bedford Square Press
26 Bedford Square
London WC1B 3HU

THE WOMEN'S DIRECTORY

Compiled by Fiona Macdonald

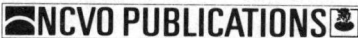

Published by
BEDFORD SQUARE PRESS of the
National Council for Voluntary Organisations
26 Bedford Square, London WC1B 3HU
© NCVO 1991

All rights reserved. No part of this publication
may be reproduced, stored in a retrieval
system or transmitted in any form or by any
means, electronic, mechanical, photocopying
or otherwise, without the prior permission of the
publisher.

Typeset by AKM Associates (UK) Ltd, Southall, London
Printed and bound in England by JW Arrowsmith Ltd, Bristol

Cover printed by Heyford Press, Wellingborough

British Library Cataloguing in Publication Data
Macdonald, Fiona
　The women's directory.
　1. Great Britain. Women's organizations
　I. Title
　305.4

ISBN 0-7199-1250-4

Contents

Foreword	vii
Acknowledgements	viii
Introduction	ix
How to use this directory	xi
Directory of women's organisations	1
Appendices	
1 Umbrella bodies	67
2 Women's centres	69
3 Crisis organisations	71
4 Political organisations	73
5 International women's organisations	75
6 Women in rural areas	77
7 Women and the family	81
8 Women and health	83
9 Women and history	85
10 Women and the media	87
11 Women and work	91
12 Finding out	93
13 Organisations which can help you set up a new group	95
Form for new directory entries	97
Classified index	99

Foreword

A desire and need to break down barriers, whether created by ignorance, isolation or exclusivity, is the hallmark of the women's world today.

Women's lives are increasingly filled with so many activities and responsibilities – both public and private, in paid or unpaid work, or both – that there is a growing awareness of the need to work together. Women also feel an increasing desire to support and sustain each other in every way possible. I therefore welcome and recommend this directory as it will help to meet these needs by offering easy access to so many women's organisations.

As we are painfully aware, one of the most difficult and essential goals to achieve in the voluntary sector is speedy, effective and sure means of communication. Good communications, a vital ingredient in modern-day life, rely on a combination of high-tech and traditional methods, requiring an adequate supply of time, personnel and funding – all precious and scarce commodities. This excellent directory will undoubtedly provide a useful and speedy means of communication at very reasonable cost.

The material in this book encompasses a wide variety of interest and is clearly set out enabling easy use. Not only are nearly 400 organisations listed, but the useful appendices provide contacts for women in rural areas, women in the media, women and the family and many more special categories besides. The directory, the fourth in the series, presenting so much information listed in one place, will be of particular value to women's organisations who do not have the time or resources to undertake research on so many subjects themselves. It is often said that it is not what you know but who you know! This directory will enable the user to contact the right person at the right time; will enlarge the organisation's network; and will facilitate contact at local, national and international levels and so enable us all to improve the range of services we can offer our members, clients and supporters.

Knowledge is power and we need each other especially now when women and their organisations are subject to the pressures of social and economic change.

Well done, and thank you NCVO!

ROSALIND PRESTON
Past President,
National Council of Women of Great Britain

Acknowledgements

As explained in the Introduction to this directory, women's organisations move, amalgamate and disappear with astonishing frequency. The publishers and compiler of **The Women's Directory** are therefore exceptionally grateful to all those individuals and organisations who have helped them with their research. Particular thanks are due to Jane Grant and her colleagues at the National Alliance of Women's Organisations for all their support, advice and information. The directory also benefited from discussions with staff of the Equal Opportunities Commission at an early planning stage, and from information and advice offered by the Information and Technology Team at NCVO, and by the staff of various women's centres.

Acknowledgements are also due to the following individuals for their help: additional research, Elizabeth Campbell; database management and production, Lynne Jarché; data preparation, Jahanara Choudry, Anne Pollard and Jane Key; editorial co-ordination, Jackie Sallon and Carole Fries; and index, Susan Bates.

Introduction

Now, more than ever before, women's organisations are busy - busy providing contact and support to women feeling isolated, unwell or confused, busy campaigning for changes or improvements in the law and in national and local government services as they affect women, busy bringing the aspirations and resentments of women into the limelight, busy researching into women's lives in the past, or into their needs - at home and in the workplace - for now and for the future. This directory of women's organisations reflects all these aspects of women's activity, and more. It can help you make contact with women who share your needs or concerns, seek help from women who will understand your problems and have the skills to try and alleviate them, or join with women to take action to improve our lives.

A great many women's organisations exist, in all corners of the British Isles. Yet finding out about them is not easy. That is why we have compiled this directory. As well as describing nearly 400 women's organisations, it also suggests how you might find out about other organisations not listed here. Various 'umbrella' organisations have collections of information about women's groups (you can find a list of them in appendix I), but there is no one, consolidated, all-embracing list which is easily available to everyone interested in women, their needs and their concerns. Indeed, it is impossible that there ever could be - although some of the data banks collected by the umbrella organisations are quite impressive.

Women's organisations are constantly changing; many are purely local, or designed to meet a particular need. When their immediate aim has been achieved, or if their local cause is taken up by some larger, more powerful body, then the reason for their existence is gone, and they fade away. Other organisations merge together, or split into a variety of smaller groups. Unfortunately, some organisations have to cease their activities through lack of funds. And many organisations rely on the energy and commitment of a few individuals. If their work or family circumstances change, or if they no longer have the free time to devote to the group, then, sadly, it often has to close down.

We hope that this directory will enable you to make contact with the women's organisation you are seeking. Be patient and persistent; if you look hard and long enough, you will almost certainly find someone to share your interests or your worries. We know that many more organisations exist than are listed in this directory. We sent them questionnaires but, whether through lack of time, shortage of funds, or the wish to ensure a degree of privacy to their members and workers, they declined to return them. We hope that they will prove more responsive to individual enquirers. The organisations that we have listed have proved that they will respond; many of them may also be able to refer you to other, related organisations, or to local groups active in your area.

If an organisation to meet your own, individual needs is not listed here, make use of 'networking'. That is, locate one source of information - such as one of the umbrella bodies of the National Alliance of Women's Organisations. NAWO, which went independent from the National Council for Voluntary Organisations in May 1989 and by September 1990 had grown to a powerful alliance of 185 organisations, keeps a database on its expanding membership. One of its functions is to help women's organisations network with each other. Or you can get in touch with a local women's centre, a council for voluntary service, or a well-established national organisation related to your own particular interests, and ask them for a few contacts. Then follow these contacts up, and ask them, in turn, for other sources of information. You might be surprised where your enquiries lead, and how many like-minded women you find within a small radius of your home or workplace. Your local reference library might also be a good place to start. You will probably find there several reference books designed to help women with young children, or women returning to work, or girls seeking an adventurous career. All of them will probably include a list of useful organisations to contact, as well as containing much useful advice.

You can also help us to make future editions of this directory more comprehensive. We have included a form at the back of this book on which information about organisations not included here can be recorded. If you are working for an organisation that is not listed here, or even if you just know of one which you feel should be included, then please complete the form and send it to us at Bedford Square Press. We will not use any information without first checking it with the organisation concerned.

How to use this directory

This directory is arranged in two main parts: subject entries and appendices. The subject entries are listed in alphabetical order; each entry gives basic information about the aims and activities of an organisation, how to contact it, and what services it provides. Each entry is arranged according to a standard pattern:

Name
Address
Person to contact
Description of aims and activities
Symbols giving further information about the organisation

Key to symbols

- * affiliated to NCVO
- † unable to trace
- C registered charity or exempted from registration
- B branches/local groups
- V volunteers welcomed
- Y young (under 18) volunteers welcomed
- M size of membership
- S number of paid staff (full- and part-time)
- L library or information room (not always open to the public; please enquire first)
- T subsidiary trading company
- P produces publications

The appendices provide a compendium of information for anyone seeking to find out more about topics and issues of interest to women. They also offer a number of contact points of particular importance to women. For example, appendix 3 lists 'crisis' numbers, while appendix 4 contains information about women and politics, and appendix 6 gives detailed information that will interest women living in rural areas. (See the contents for a full list of the appendices.)

At the end of the book, in appendix 13, is a list of organisations which can help if you want to set up a new organisation, or if you are seeking advice on how to make your own organisation operate more effectively and efficiently.

There is a classified subject index, which will enable readers searching for help to locate an organisation which can offer advice on, for example, the problems of breast-feeding, or the difficulty of training for a male-related career.

There is also a blank form (with permission to be photocopied) on which we hope readers will send in information to help us prepare an enlarged edition of this directory in the future.

Criteria for inclusion

The organisations listed in this directory are all 'voluntary' (interpreted as meaning a self-governing body of people who have joined together for the betterment of the community, and not for financial gain) or else not-for-profit and/or co-operative bodies. Most of these organisations are dependent on voluntary funds, sometimes supplemented by grant aid.

The exceptions to this are the public bodies, political parties women's sections, bookshops and publications listed in appendices 1, 4 and 12. We have included these because we feel that they can all serve as valuable sources of information for women, and have all offered help, of various kinds, to women in recent years.

Most of the organisations listed here are countrywide in character, or are regarded as leading bodies in their field and are prepared to respond to enquiries from anywhere in the country. We have not included information about women's organisations concerned exclusively with women living in Scotland, Wales and Northern Ireland. Information about these organisations may be obtained from the appropriate 'umbrella' bodies listed in appendix 1, or from one of the relevant women's centres listed in appendix 2.

Accuracy of contents

Bedford Square Press and the National Council of

Voluntary Organisations cannot accept responsibility for statements made in this directory. The particulars are based on information supplied by the organisations concerned, or taken from their own published material, edited where necessary to standardise presentation. While every effort has been made to ensure that details are accurate and up to date, some changes in office-holders or addresses may occur before publication. We should be grateful if any such changes could be notified to us, so that we may make any necessary alterations to the text in future editions.

Contacting a voluntary organisation

There has only been space to include a brief amount of information about each organisation. If you would like to find out more, or if you wish to join one of the organisations listed here, or to offer your help, please write or telephone them directly. Many voluntary organisations are chronically short of funds. This applies particularly to women's organisations, which are often run on the proverbial shoestring, so please send a large stamped addressed envelope with your enquiry, and do not be surprised if it takes the organisation a little time to reply. Many organisations rely almost entirely on voluntary help, and hard-pressed volunteer workers can at times find themselves faced with a mountain of paperwork after a busy week in the factory or office, or while coping with the demands of a home and family. And, while many voluntary organisations generously offer free advice leaflets and factsheets to enquirers, you should be prepared to pay for more substantial publications. Most organisations will be happy to send you a free list of the books and other materials they produce.

300 Group
36-37 Charterhouse Square, London EC1M 6EA
071-600 2390 Fax 071-600 2391
Contact Kathy Bell
Campaigns for greater participation by women in public life and an equal balance of male and female MPs in the House of Commons. Also aims to empower women through its training programmes to have the confidence to seek public office.
* C B V(Y) M(1,000+) S(1) P

35's Women's Campaign for Soviet Jewry (35's)
Pannell House, 779-781 Finchley Road, London NW11 8DN
081-458 7148
Contact Joyce Simson
Publicises violations of human rights in the Soviet Union. Lobbies MPs, trade unions, churches, synagogues and schools in order to bring these matters to the attention of the public.

Abortion Law Reform Association (ALRA)
88 Islington High Street, London N1 8EG
071-359 5200
Contact Hilary Jackson
Seeks to achieve a woman's right to choose, in law and in practice, whether or not to continue a pregnancy. Campaigns and runs educational activities; disseminates information.
B V M(1,000) P

Academic Women's Achievement Group (AWAG)
c/o Professor Hannah Steinberg, Kathleen Lonsdale Building, University College London, Gower Street, London WC1E 6BT
071-380 7232
Contact Hannah Steinberg
Seeks to remedy the under-representation of women academics in universities and the tendency for them to remain at the lower end of the career structure. Holds regular meetings with guest speakers to gather facts, keep up with current events affecting women in higher education and to draw the results of these activities to the attention of decision-makers.
M(100) P

Acceptance Helpline and Support Group for Parents of Lesbians and Gay Men (Acceptance)
64 Holmside Avenue, Halfway Houses, Sheerness, Kent ME12 3EY
0795-661463
Contact Jill Green
Runs a telephone helpline (Tues-Fri 7.00 pm-9.00 pm) for parents concerned about their son's or daughter's homosexuality. Organises a support group for parents; meetings currently based in Kent but expansion possible.
B V P

Active Birth Centre (ABC)
55 Dartmouth Park Road, London NW5 1SL
071-267 3006 Fax 071-267 5368
Contact Janet Balaskas
Provides free national and international information service on all aspects of active birth. Runs workshops and classes for couples preparing for an active birth or water birth; teacher-training course for active birth teachers; yoga for

pregnancy. Hires and sells water-birth pools. Mail order catalogue available.
B V M(50) S(4) T(Active Birth Sales) P

Afro-Caribbean Educational Project - Women's Centre (ACEP - Women's Centre)
603 High Road, Leyton, London E10 6RF
081-556 4053
Contact Veronica Roach
The Women's Centre provides facilities for African and Caribbean women and their children. The Educational Project offers activities which will help to advance the general development of all users and members of the centre.
C V S(4) P

Agoraphobia Information Service
4 Manorbrook, London SE3 9AW
081-318 5026
Contact Alice Neville
Provides information about agoraphobia and general anxiety states; establishes contacts between self-help organisations and between individual sufferers; runs telephone helpline.
P

Al-Anon Family Groups
61 Great Dover Street, London SE1 4YF
071-403 0888
Provides understanding and support for relatives and friends of problem drinkers, whether or not the alcoholic is still drinking. Also runs Alateen, to help people aged 12-18 who are, or have been, affected by an alcoholic relative. Runs over 1000 groups throughout the UK and Eire.
C B V P

Alcohol Counselling Service
34 Electric Lane, London SW9 8JT
071-737 3570   01-737 3579
Contact Juliette Small
Provides a one-to-one counselling service for anyone who is experiencing problems associated with alcohol and for their relatives or friends.
C B V P

Alcoholics Anonymous (AA)
General Service Office, PO Box 1, Stonebow House, Stonebow, York YO1 2NJ
0904-644026 (admin)
071-352 3001 (helpline10 am-10 pm)
Fax 0904-629091
Maintains nationwide network of local groups of people who wish to achieve and maintain sobriety by staying away from alcoholic drinks. Most groups run open meetings once a week, and any interested member of the public is welcome to attend.
C B P

Anorexia and Bulimia Nervosa Association
Tottenham Women's Health Centre, Annexe C, Tottenham Town Hall, Town Hall Approach, London N15 4RX
081-885 3936(helpline, Weds 6 pm - 9 pm)
Contact Clare Dyas
Provides a confidential helpline run by women who have experience of eating problems; gives help, support and information; arranges workshops, lectures and promotional

activities nationwide to discuss the issue of women and food and to encourage the formation of local support groups.
C V P

Anorexics Anonymous
24 Westmoreland Road, London SW13 9RY
081-748 3994
Offers free counselling and advice by appointment for people suffering from anorexia nervosa, bulimia and other eating disorders.
V

Aphra Videos
The Diorama, 14 Peto Place, London NW1 4DT
071-987 3224
Contact Rebecca Maguire
Takes particular interest in working with women's groups, running training workshops for girls and women in basic video production skills, scriptwriting and pre-production at basic and intermediate level. Training is prioritised for minority ethnic women as a means of redressing their current under-representation in media employment.
V(Y) M(8) S(3) T(Aphra Videos) P

Asian Young Women's Project (AYWP)
8 Manor Gardens, London N7 6JZ
071-263 6270
Contact Asmat Hussain
Enables Asian young women (aged 11-25) to make positive choices about their lives by offering advice, counselling, support and youth activities. Answers enquiries from anywhere in the country.
C B V(Y) M(30) S(3) P

Associated Country Women of the World
Vincent House, Vincent Square, London SW1P 2NB
071-834 8635
Contact J J Pearce
Aims to raise the general standard of living of women and their families all over the world by working for the relief of poverty and sickness and promoting the advancement of education.
C B V M(9m) S(10) P

Association for Improvements in the Maternity Services
40 Kingswood Avenue, London NW6 6LS
081-960 5585
Contact Sandar Warshal
Offers advice and information to parents on all aspects of pregnancy and childbirth.
B V M(1,000+) P

Association for Post-Natal Illness
7 Gowan Avenue, London SW6 6RH
071-731 4867
Contact Sheila Hamblett
Maintains a register of volunteers who have suffered and recovered from post-natal depression. Supports a depressed mother on a one-to-one basis.
C B V P

Association of Breastfeeding Mothers
Order Department, Sydenham Green Health Centre, Holmshaw Close, London SE26 4TH
081-778 4769
Contact Elizabeth Dudley
Promotes the physical and psychological health of mothers and children through education in the techniques of breastfeeding; advances public education on the health benefits of breastfeeding. The association is dedicated to making breastfeeding a successful and happy experience for all mothers who choose it, and has support groups throughout the UK.
C B V M(300) P

Association of Lawyers for the Defence of the Unborn (ALDU)
40 Bedford Street, London WC2E 9EN
Campaigns to oppose abortion; acts as an educational body within the legal profession on this issue; opposes any pro-abortion changes in the law; campaigns to create a climate of opinion in the legal profession in favour full statutory protection for the unborn.
M(2,000) P

Association of Radical Midwives (ARM)
62 Greetby Hill, Ormskirk, Lancs L39 2DT
0695-572776
Contact Ishbel Karger
Works to improve maternity services, especially within the NHS; campaigns to preserve and enhance choices in childbirth for all women and to re-establish the full role of midwives.
* B M(890) S(1) P

Association of Women Solicitors (1919 Club)
The Law Society, 50-52 Chancery Lane, London WC2A 1SX
071-242 1222 Fax 071-405 9522
Contact Judith McDermott
Body within the Law Society which aims to develop policies promoting the interests of women solicitors.
B P

Baby Life Support Systems (BLISS)
17-21 Emerald Street, London WC1N 3QL
071-831 9393 Fax 071-404 0676
Contact Judy Kay
Aims to ensure that every baby has an equal chance in life, and that no baby dies or suffers handicap because vital equipment and skilled care are not available during the critical first moments of life.
* C B V M(950) S(2)

Baby Milk Action (BMAC)
6 Regent Terrace, Cambridge CB2 1AA
0223-464420 Fax 0223-464417
Contact Patti Rundall
Promotes breastfeeding and other practices beneficial to the health and welfare of infants and young children and their families, and discourages irresponsible marketing of artificial infant feeding products. Promotes public education and the spread of information, knowledge and ideas; sponsors and organises workshops,

seminars, meetings, etc; also conducts research and seeks funds.
* B V(Y) M(500) S(4) P

Baha'i National Women's Committee
27 Rutland Gate, London SW7 1PD
0732-462328 071-584 2566
Fax 0732-462849
Contact Lois Hainsworth
Aims to develop throughout the UK an awareness of the Baha'i teachings on the emancipation of women and the achievement of full equality between the sexes. Promotes the involvement of Baha'i women in the social, civic and religious life of the community and demonstrates their commitment to the oneness of mankind and the fundamental oneness of religion.
C B M(2,500) V P

Bangladesh Women's Association
91 Highbury Hill, London N5 1SX
071-359 5836
Contact Aleya Rozina
Offers help and advice on matters of housing, social security and unemployment benefits, pensions and widow's allowance, immigration and nationality, employment training, health and child care, etc. Provides courses and leisure activities; ESL, sewing and music classes; weekend classes for children.
C B V

Beaumont Society
PO Box 3084, London WC1N 3XX
Offers help, information and advice to transvestites and transsexuals, and free information to all enquirers. Also arranges social meetings, and runs a support group for wives and partners.

Counselling can be arranged via the Beaumont Trust.
B M(700) P

Birth Control Campaign
27-35 Mortimer Street, London W1N 7RJ
071-580 9360
Contact Madelaine Tearse
Promotes the optimum provision of birth control services within the National Health Service, including voluntary sterilisaton and abortion. Campaigns for the provision of any other services which would increase the availability of birth control facilities to the individual. Promotes education and publicity for a responsible attitude to contraception.
S(1)

Birth Control Trust
27-35 Mortimer Street, London W1N 7RJ
071-580 9360
Contact Madeleine Tearse
Supports good public provision of contraception, sterilisation and abortion services in Britain. Provides information and research on birth control, specialising in abortion.
* C S(1) P

Birthright (National Fund for Childbirth Research)
27 Sussex Place, Regents Park, London NW1 4SP
071-723 9296
Contact Vivienne Parry
Funds medical research for the better health of women and babies; funds research and the development of new treatments for a wide range of gynaecological and obstetric problems, especially those

encountered before, during and after birth.
* C B V S(6) T(Birthright Trading Ltd) P

Black Female Prisoners Scheme
Brixton Enterprise Centre,
444 Brixton Road, London SW9 8HE
071-733 5520
Contact Sherine Thompson
Provides a service reintroducing the offender back into the community. Offers help with social services, family, housing and customs to women in prison and on their release. Writes to families and organisations overseas on behalf of clients.
S(6) M

Black Women for Wages for Housework (BWWFH)
King's Cross Women's Centre,
71 Tonbridge Street, London WC1H 9DZ
071-837 7509
Contact Wilmette Brown
Network of black/Third World women aiming to dismantle both racism and sexism by having all unwaged work of women counted in the GNP and claiming reparations for slavery, imperialism and neo-colonialism. Unites black, Third World, women's, class and green issues by campaigning on welfare, immigration controls, police illegality, rape, prostitution, health and disability, nuclear power/weapons and ecology.
B V(Y) P

Break
20 Hooks Hill Road, Sheringham, Norfolk NR26 8NL
0263-823170 Fax 0263-823995
Contact Geoffrey Davison
Provides holidays, short-stay and emergency care throughout the year for handicapped adults and children (accompanying adults accepted), irrespective of degree of disability. Escort facilities available.
* C B V S(48) P

Breast Cancer Research Trust
7 Soho Street, London W1V 5FA
071-734 1882/3
Contact Anthea Barlow
Aims to prevent and find a cure for breast cancer.
C B V S(1)

Breast Care and Mastectomy Association of Great Britain
26a Harrison Street, London WC1H 8JG
071-837 0908
Contact Andrea Whalley
Offers emotional support and practical information to complement medical advice and nursing.
* C V S(4) T P

Bristol Association for Neighbourhood Daycare
43 Ducie Road, Barton Hill, Bristol BS5 0AX
0272-556971 0272-542128
Contact Sue Richards
Promotes neighbourhood-based daycare schemes, especially those for school-age children of working parents, recognising in particular the needs of single parents. Raises funds to assist new local groups to organise holiday and afterschool

schemes. Publishes information to guide local groups, provides advisory support; acts as a vehicle for sharing information and resources.
C P

British Association for Betterment of Infertility and Education (BABIE)
PO Box 4TS, London W1A 4TS
071-224 4724 0278-683595
Fax 071-224 4725
Contact Secretary
Offers advice and counselling to people with infertility problems. Provides treatment at cost price for vitro fertilisation (test tube baby) and artificial insemination, etc. Produces factsheets; runs telephone hotline for members.
C P

British Association of Women Entrepreneurs (BAWE)
Inigo House, 29 Bedford Street, Covent Garden, London WC2E 9RT
071-379 3385 Fax 071-497 9249
Contact Katia Lewis
British arm of les Femmes Chefs d'Entreprise Mondiale; aims to bring together women who are 'heads of business'; takes an active part in employers' organisations. Holds regular meetings in London and international conferences.
V S(2) P

British Federation of University Women
Crosby Hall, Cheyne Walk, London SW3 5BA
071-352 5354
Contact Eileen Menzies
Maintains an organisation which represents university women in all professions, and enables them to take concerted action
B

British Housewives' League (BHL)
c/o Honorary Secretary, 24 Liverpool Road, Kingston Hill, Surrey KT2 7SZ
Contact A C Horsfield
Aims to provide housewives with an effective voice in all matters concerning the welfare of themselves and their families; to achieve an ample, wholesome and affordable supply of food and a decent standard of living.
V P

British Organisation of Non-Parents (BON)
BM Box 5866, London WC1N 3XX
Contact Root Cartwright
Promotes the belief that having children should be a matter of free choice, and that the child-free option should be respected. Seeks to combat prejudices against non-parents and the pronatalist bias in society.
V M(120+) P

British Pregnancy Advisory Service (BPAS)
Austy Manor, Wootton Wawen, Solihull, West Midlands B95 6BX
05642-3225 Fax 05642-4935
Contact Diana Burt
Offers help and advice to women experiencing problems in pregnancy and provides a range of services concerned with fertility and infertility. These include pregnancy testing, contraception (including 'morning after' treatment), male and female sterilisation and its reversal, abortion,

infertility investigations and artificial insemination.
C B S(460) P

Brittle Bone Society
112 City Road, Dundee DD2 2PW
0382-817771
Raises funds for the support and encouragement of research into the causes, inheritance and management of brittle bones. Advises on sources of accurate genetic advice and allows patients and relatives of patients with these disorders to get in contact and exchange information.
C B V M(1,396) S(4) P

Brook Advisory Centres
153a East Street, London SE17 2SD
071-708 1390
Contact Alison Hadley Offers free contraceptive advice and supplies to young people, also pregnancy testing, pregnancy counselling, and counselling for sexual and emotional problems. For details of your nearest centre, telephone 071-708 1234.
* C B M(160) S(500) P

Brothers and Sisters Club
109 Kessock Close, Ferry Lane Estate, Tottenham London N17 9PW
Social club with monthly meetings for deaf lesbians and gay men.
P

Caesarian Support Group of Cambridge
81 Elizabeth Way, Cambridge
CB4 1BQ
0223-314211
Contact Diane Barnes
Supports and advises (non-medically) women who have had or are about to have a caesarian birth. Runs local groups, and can advise on how to start one if necessary. Publishes a handbook for parents.
B V P

Campaign Against Pornography
96 Dalston Lane, London E8 1NG
071-923 4303
Contact Sam Chugg
Campaigns to raise public awareness about the direct links between pornography and sexual violence in all its forms and to expose the damage done by pornography. The involvement of women is a priority. Encourages action against the distribution of pornographic material.
C B V P

Campaign Against Pornography and Censorship (CPC)
PO Box 844, London SE5 9QP
071-274 3072
Contact Catherine Itzin
Opposes pornography on the grounds that it contributes to sexual violence and sex discrimination, and infringes the civil liberties of women. CPC is campaigning for the legislation against pronography without censorship, using a Sex Discrimination Ac t model and a Race Relations Act model of

incitement to sexual hatred and violence.
V P

Campaign for Homosexual Equality (CHE)
38 Mount Pleasant, London WC1X 0AP
071-833 3912
Aims for social and legal equality for homosexual and bisexual women and men. Drafts amendments to the law and campaigns for their adoption.
V B P

Campaign for Press and Broadcasting Freedom (CPBF)
The Unity Club, 96 Dalston Lane, London E8 1NG
071-923 3671 Fax 071-923 3672
Contact Mick Gosling
Distributes media codes of conduct on racism and sexism. Lobbies for statutory Right of Reply and advises those suffering from media distortion. Monitors and advises on current media legislation. Organises meetings, conferences, schools and exhibitions on media issues. Produces videos and publications.
B V M(1,500) S(2) P

Capital Helpline Services
Euston Tower, London NW1 3DR
071-388 7575 (9.30am-5.30pm, Mon-Fri)
Confidential off-air advice and information service, staffed by counsellors with a wide range of experience and expertise. Helpline is delighted to hear from anyone with any sort of problem, great or small. They will listen, advise and put you in touch with other relevant organisations when appropriate.

Careers for Women
4th Floor, 2 Valentine Place, London SE1 8QH 071-401 2280
Fax 071-401 2938
Contact Kalyani Menon
Offers interviews to girls and women of all ages; runs courses; produces and sells literature; answers questions on careers by post.
C M(150) S(6) P

Catholic Aids Link (CAL)
PO Box 646, London E9 6QP
081-986 0807
Contact Martin Pendergast
Catholic support group offering non-judgemental, spiritual, emotional, practical and financial help to those people affected by HIV/AIDS. Maintains a network throughout England, Wales, Scotland and Ireland and has strong international contacts. Aims to enlist the resources of the RC church in England and Wales to increase awareness about the condition.
B V M(450) P

Catholic Marriage Advisory Council
Clitherow House, 1 Blythe Mews, Blythe Road, London W14 0NW
071-371 1341
Contact Stuart W G Ritchie
Trained counsellors help people to prepare for, achieve and sustain successful marriages, and offer support if relationships break down.
***** **C B V M(843) S(20)**

Catholic Needlework Guild (CNG)
80 Warde Chase, Wade Reach,
Walton on the Naze, Essex
CO14 8QW
0255-850251
Contact M W Doherty
Supplies new, useful and warm clothing for those who through unfortunate circumstances are unable to provide for themselves and their families.
C B V(Y) M(4,250) P

Catholic Women's League
PO Box 621, Earls Colne,
Colchester, Essex CO6 2ST
0787-223382
Contact Joan Crossman
Unites Catholic women in a bond of common fellowship; promotes religious, educational and social welfare interests on parish, diocesan, national and international levels; ensures Catholic representation of those interests on major public bodies; initiates and maintains charitable works.
C B V M(10,000) S(1) P

Centre for Women's Studies
Coventry Polytechnic, Priory Street,
Coventry CV1 5FB
0203-838336
Contact Helen Matthews
The centre co-ordinates research and teaching in women's studies, holds seminars and summer/day schools, runs access courses for women wishing to re-enter education or work.
C V P

Cervical Stitch Network
Fairfield, Wolverton Road, Norton Lindsey, Warwicks CV35 8LA
092684-3223
Contact Julie Howard
Provides information, advice, support and local contacts for women who need, or might need, a cervical stitch in pregnancy. Produces leaflets and booklet.
C(Miscarriage Association) V M(400) P

Change International Reports: Women and Society (Change)
PO Box 824, London SE24 9JS
071-277 6187
Contact Georgina Ashworth
Publishes material on the status of women in different countries and campaigns to improve their position.
C V S(1) P

CHAT
Royal College of Nursing,
20 Cavendish Square, London
W1M 0AB
071-629 3870
Contact Colin Somerville
Offers a personal, confidential counselling service for all nurses on a self-referral basis. Counsellors visit locations around Britain.
C B P

Child
PO Box 154, Hounslow, Middx
TW5 0EZ
081-571 4367
Contact Clare Brown
Assists in the development of research into the causes of infertility. Helps people suffering from infertility by educating them in methods of

overcoming their disability. Provides counselling services for their benefit.
C B V M(1,040) S(1) P

Child Poverty Action Group (CPAG)
1-5 Bath Street, London EC1V 9PY
071-253 3406
Contact Fran Bennett
Carries out research and campaigns against poverty in families with children.
***** C B V M(6,000) S(21) T(CPAG Ltd) P**

Chile Solidarity Campaign Women's Section
129 Seven Sisters Road, London N7 7QG
O71-272 4298
Contact Diane Dixon
Aims to support and publicise the women's movement in Chile and especially to support women's projects. Raises money for development projects in health and childcare. Maintains and extends links with women in Chile. Runs greeting card campaigns to support women's organisations and women political prisoners.
P

Chiswick Family Rescue Ltd
PO Box 855, London W4 4JF
081-747 0133 (office) 081-995 4430 (crisis line)
Provides accommodation and support for women escaping violence. Runs a 24-hour crisis line and provides nursery facilities for children living in the refuges.
P

Christian Women's Information and Resources (CWIRES)
Blackfriars, St Giles, Oxford OX1 3LY
0865-516*218*
Contact Katie Hambrook
Provides a library and information service for and about women and the church. Members may borrow from the library, and receive regular newsletters with news of Christian feminist groups and events plus book reviews. Visits to CWIRES may be made by a ppointment.
C V M(200) L P

Cinema of Women (COW)
31 Clerkenwell Close, London EC1R 0AT
071-251 4978
Contact Jenny Wallace
Distributes films and videos produced by women to as wide an audience as possible.
M(8) S(2) P

City Centre
32-35 Featherstone Street, London EC1Y 8QX
071-608 1338
Contact Rohan Collier
Provides information, advice and resources for office workers on matters of employment rights, equal opportunities and health and safety, including VDU hazards and women's health. Publishes information packs, factsheets and newsletters.
M(220) S(4) P

City Women's Network
925 Uxbridge Road, Hillingdon
Heath, Middx UB10 0NJ
081-569 2351
Fax 081-569 2352
Contact Jeanette Masarati
Networking forum for professional women; encourages and promotes the contributions made by professional women to business and relevant personal issues. Also provides a full programme of business, social and educational events; and produces a monthly newsletter.
V M(200+) P

Co-operative Women's Guild
342 Hoe Street, Walthamstow,
London E17 9PX
081-520 4902
Contact National President
Educates women in the principles and practice of the co-operative; encourages and prepares women to play a greater part in community, national and international affairs. Also works for the establishment of world peace.
B V P

Concern for Family and Womanhood - Campaign for the Feminine Woman (CFW)
Springfield House, Chedworth, Cheltenham, Glos GL54 4AH
0285-720454
Contact Yvonne Stayt
Promotes and advances education in the different sex roles, marriage and the family in accordance with the Bible and nature. Promotes the value and validity of the dominant responsible masculine man and the submissive feminine woman and her important natural role of wife and mother in the home. Important to both men and women, the CFW demands an end to feminist legislation, education, propaganda, attitudes, etc.
C V M(2,000) P

Conservative Women's National Committee
32 Smith Square, London
SW1P 3HH
071-222 9000
Contact Jane Garrett
Co-ordinates the work of the area women's committees and acts as a two-way channel of communication, advice and guidance between the constituencies and national level. Considers resolutions, reports and communications from all women's committees of t he Party.
B V P

Copper 7 Association
28 Finlay Gardens, Addlestone, Weybridge, Surrey KT15 2XN
Contact Jeanette Morris
Provides a contact group for women suffering from problems when using the Copper 7 IUD. Publicises the risks to all users and follows up possible claims in court against the manufacturers. If enough evidence is forthcoming, considers campaigning to remove Copper 7 from the market.
V M(80) P

Courtney Foundation for the Welfare of Mothers and Babies (WOMB)
33 Harley Street, London W1N 1DA
071-323 0090
Contact Dr Tom Courtney
Medical charity that addresses the special medical and psychological problems of chemical addiction and HIV infection in women, in pregnancy and in the new-born. WOMB's philosophy is to delivery babies drug-free and disease-free. Aims to provide women with a one-door point of entry to a continuum of appropriate medical and social services which can be made available to them without stigma as their personal needs arise.
C V P

Creative and Supportive Trust (CAST)
37-39 Kings Terrace, London NW1 0JR
071-383 5228
Contact Helen Taylor
Provides support and information and runs workshops (based in London) for women and girls who have experienced imprisonment or detention of various kinds, in prisons, psychiatric units, foster homes and similar institutions, and those on probation.
* C V S(8) P

CREW
Rue Stevin 38, 1040 Brussels, Belgium
010 32 2-230 51 58
Contact R Franceskides
Independent women's co-operative offering consultancy in areas of policy affecting women. Undertakes research; publishes a monthly magazine offering a critical view on European social, employment and training policy. Co-ordinates IRIS, a European net work of vocational training schemes for women, for the European Commission.
P

Crisis Counselling for Alleged Shoplifters (CCAS)
PO Box 1892, London NW4 4NX
081-202 5787 (24-hour answering machine) 081-958 8859 (after 7pm)
Contact Regina Dollar
Provides counselling, advice and support to people accused of alleged shoplifting offences; has particular concern for the problems of children. Refers cases to professionals where necessary; liaises with and lobbies MPs, local authorities and other organisations to discuss relevant aspects of social, political and legal policy or practice and procedure.
B V

Cruse - Bereavement Care
Cruse House, 126 Sheen Road, Richmond, Surrey TW9 1UR
081-940 4818
Contact Alec Sandison
Offers a service of counselling, advice and opportunities for social contact to all bereaved people.
* C B V M(15,000) S(25) P

CRY-SIS Support Group
BM CRY-SIS, London WC1N 3XX
071-404 5011
Contact Fiona Webb
Helps and supports parents of excessively crying/or sleepless babies and young children. Provides

literature for parents and professionals.
C B V M(300) P

Cypriot Women's League
376 St Anne's Road, London N15 3JL
081-800 8398
Deals with women's rights; offers advice and help on welfare rights, conditions for homeworkers.
B P

Cystitis and Candida
75 Mortimer Road, London N1 5AR
071-249 8664
Contact Angela Kilmartin
Provides information (classes and books), lectures and one-to-one counselling to help prevent and manage these problems. Offers telephone advice; holds group meetings.
P

Dalkon Shield Association
24 Patshull Road, London NW5 2JY
071-485 7743 (8-9 pm for enquiries only)
Informal group of volunteers who offer information about Dalkon Shields and help people who are taking legal action against the manufacturers.

Day Care Trust/National Childcare Campaign Ltd
Wesley House, 4 Wild Court, London WC2B 5AU
071-405 5617
Provides information to parents about childcare issues. Promotes the development of high-quality childcare services. Provides telephone and written information for parents and providers. Establishes new information and development centres nationally.
B V M(35) S(4) P

Divorce Conciliation and Advisory Service (DCAS)
38 Ebury Street, London SW1W 0LU
071-730 2422
Contact Hilary Halpin
Offers help to parents to maintain workable arrangements for themselves and their children. Also offers counselling to individuals prior to divorce or post-divorce.
C V M(6) S(1)

Drugs, Alcohol, Women, Now (DAWN)
Omnibus Workspace, 39-41 North Road, London N7 9DP
071-700 4653
Provides information to women on drug and alcohol-related issues. Promotes awareness of women's needs amongst agencies; the development of services; public and professional education.
* C M(9) S(4) P

Eating Disorders Association (formerly Anorexic Aid and Anorexic Family Aid)
Sackville Place, 44 Magdalen Street, Norwich NR3 1JE
0603-621414
Contact Joanna Vincent
Offers support and mutual self care to those suffering from anorexia and bulimia nervosa and their families through telephone helplines, a network of self-help groups, information and newsletters. For advice about education and self-help

groups contact The Priory Centre, 11 Priory Road, High Wycombe, Bucks HP13 6SL, tel 0494-21431.
* C B V M(2,500) S(7) P

Elizabeth Garrett Anderson Action Committee
c/o 26 Merryweather Court, Poynings Road, London N19 5LF
071-229 9248
Contact Judi Wilson
Campaigns to restore the Elizabeth Garrett Anderson Hospital as a hospital where women can be guaranteed services directly provided by women doctors, nurses and other staff; and for the hospital to remain on its present site as a separate women-for-women service.
V

Embroiderers' Guild
Apartment 41, Hampton Court Palace, East Molesey, Surrey KT8 9AU
081-943 1229
Contact Ann Joyce
Promotes the craft of embroidery; membership open to anyone interested in embroidery from beginner to expert. 143 branches throughout the UK offer classes, lectures, exhibitions, conferences, seminars, regional events; also Young Embroiderers' Society. Publishes quarterly magazine.
C B V M(10,250) S(10) T(E G Enterprises Ltd) P

Endometriosis Society
65 Holmdene Avenue, London SE24 9LD
071-737 4764 (evenings)
Gives support to sufferers and puts them in touch with others. Provides information and advice.
C B V M(3,000) P

English Collective of Prostitutes (ECP)
c/o King's Cross Women's Centre, 71 Tonbridge Street, London WC1H 9DZ
071-837 7501
Contact Nina Lopez-Jones
Campaigns and lobbies Parliament to bring about changes in legislation relating to prostitution. Supports a network of women of different races working at various levels of the sex industry.
V P

European Forum of Socialist Feminists - UK Group
c/o Garden Flat, 7 Acol Road, London NW6 3AA
071-328 5108
Contact Clare Crocker
UK section of a Europe-wide organisation which aims to create links among women and to campaign for better representation and involvement of women at all levels of political, social and cultural life.
P

Everywoman Publishing Ltd
34 Islington Green, London N1 8DU
071-359 5496
Contact Christine George
Publishes a monthly news and current affairs magazine for and by women.
P

Exploring Parenthood
39-41 North Road, London N7 9DP
071-607 9647
Contact Carolyn Douglas
Offers support, advice and counselling to parents experiencing difficulties in the family. Runs day workshops, training scheme for parent support group leaders, and telephone advice line.
*C B V P

FAEERU (Women's Group)
116 Ladbroke Grove, London
W10 5NE
071-221 2007
Contact Josefina de Alba
Offers information and advice on matters relating to welfare benefits, education, immigration, etc. particularly for people who speak Spanish including those from Latin America or Morocco;
Monday-Saturday 3.30 - 8 pm.
V P

Families Need Fathers
BM Families, London WC1N 3XX
081-886 0970
Contact David Cannon
Provides advice, support and group counselling to parents of both sexes who do not have custody of their children. Local groups throughout the country. 'Walk-in Talk-in' sessions in Conway Hall, Red Lion Square, London WC1, from 7.30-9.30 pm on 1st and 3rd Fridays of each month.
C M(400) P

Family Cancer Clinic
Royal Free Hospital, Clinical Genetics Department, Pond Street, London NW3 2QG
071-794 0500
Contact Dr K MacDermot
A clinic for families with concern about increased risk of cancer. Open to siblings and offspring of patients with premenopausal breast cancer, colorectal cancer under the age of 50, or families with multiple cancers. Risks estimated from family trees, and appropriate screening offered. Referrals from family doctors, or self-referrals welcome. Publishes articles in scientific journals.
P

Family Planning Association
Margaret Pyke House, 27-35 Mortimer Street, London W1N 7RJ
071-636 7866 Fax 071-436 3288
Contact Information Department
Promotes sexual, emotional and reproductive health including planned parenthood. Provides a public information service; offers professional training; produces publications; runs an information and resource centre.
* C B V M(900) S(65) T(Family Planning Sales) P

Family Rights Group
The Print House, 18 Ashwin Street, London E8 3DL
071-923 2628 071-249 0008 (advice 9.30-12.00 Mon, Tues, Thurs, Fri; 1.30-4.00 Wed) Fax 071-923 2683
Provides advice and representation for families with children in public care or involved in child protection procedures; trains and advises social workers, lawyers and other professionals about family and child care law and good practice; responds to central and local government proposals on family and child care policy and practice.
* C M(1,000) S(6) P

Farm Women's Club
c/o 'Farmers Weekly', Greenfield House, Manor Road, Wallington, Surrey SM6 0DE
081-661 4930 Fax 081-647 4892
Contact Judy Steele
Informal leisure and social group for women readers of 'Farmers Weekly' magazine. Organises local groups, regular meetings, fundraising for charity; produces quarterly newsletter.
B V P

Fawcett Library
City of London Polytechnic, Old Castle Street, London E1 7NT
071-247 5826
Contact David Doughan
Britain's main library on women's studies and women's history.
C V M(3,938) S(4) P

Fawcett Society
46 Harleyford Road, London SE11 5AY
071-587 1287
Contact Julia Hubble
Stands for equal rights and responsibilities between men and women as citizens. Aims for the removal of all inequalities and discrimination based on sex, whether in law, practice or custom, and the promotion of equal opportunity in all spheres of work or other endeavour.
* B V M(500) S(2)

Feed-Back
19 Powell Street, Sheffield S3 7NW
0742-756501
Contact Kass Biggin
Provides a support service for the sufferers of a wide range of eating disorders, ie Anorexia Nervosa, Bulimia Nervosa and compulsive eating. Organises self-help groups. Provides a one-to-one counselling service.
C B V M(357)

Feminist Archive
Trinity Road Library, St Phillips, Bristol BS2 0NW
0272-350025 Opening hours: Wed 2-7.30 pm, Sat 2-8 pm, or by appointment.
A collection point for women's history, mostly from 1960 onwards, and a place where women can learn about their history. The archive houses a vast range of material documenting women's lives, including 600 sets of periodicals, tapes, art manuscripts, books, ephemera, and the Dora Russell collection.
C V

Feminist Audio Books (FAB)
52-54 Featherstone Street, London
EC1Y 8RT
071-251 2908
Contact Amorette Greene
Provides tape library of books by, for and about women. The library is for anybody who is blind, partially sighted and/or has difficulty with the printed word.
V(Y) P

Feminist Library and Information Centre
5 Westminster Bridge Road, London, SE1 7XW
071-928 7789
Specialises in contemporary literature from women's liberation movements worldwide.
C V P

Foresight Charity for Preconceptual Care
The Old Vicarage, Church Lane, Witley, Godalming, Surrey GU8 5PN
0428-684500
Contact Eve Mervyn-Smith
Promotes care for both parents before conception so that problems of birth defects are tackled before they can start.
C B V P

Foundation for the Study of Infant Deaths (Cot Death Research and Support)
35 Belgrave Square, London SW1X 8QB
071-235 1721 Fax 071-823 1986
Contact Erica De'Ath
Raises funds for research into cot death; supports bereaved parents; acts as a centre of information for professionals parents and the general public.
* C B V T(FSID Sales Ltd) L P

Foundation for Women's Health, Research and Development (FORWARD)
Africa Centre, 38 King Street, London WC2E 8JT
071-379 6889
Contact Secretary
Works towards the improvement of African women's reproductive health; campaigns against female circumcision; maintains a small resource centre; disseminates information and offers counselling, workshops and telephone advice, and training for professional health workers.

Gay and Lesbian Legal Advice (GLAD)
67-69 Cowcross Street, London EC1M 6BP
071-253 2043 (Mon-Fri, 7-10 pm)
Contact Administrator
Provides a telephone service for lesbians and gay men giving both legal advice and information with regard to the way in which they are affected by the law.
V M(25) S(1)

Gay Authors Workshop (GAW)
BM Box 5700, London WC1N 3XX
Contact Kathryn Byrd
Holds monthly meetings to discuss work and share information on lesbian and gay writing; encourages new writers; produces quarterly newsletter in print and on tape.
M(30) P

Gay Bereavement Project
Unitarian Rooms, Hoop Lane,
London NW11 8BS
081-455 8894 (helpline) 081-455 6844 (admin)
Contact Dudley Cave
Offers advice and support by telephone to lesbians and gay men bereaved by the death of a life partner. Seeks to educate all people concerned with death and dying to the special problems of same-sex loss, and to educate lesbians and gay men of the need to write wills and prepare for the day when 'we' becomes 'I'.
C V M(16)

Gay Switchboard
071-837 7324
Runs a 24-hour telephone advice service for homosexual people.

Gemma (Lesbians with/without Disabilities)
BM Box 5700, London WC1N 3XX
Contact Elsa Beckett
Lessens the isolation of disabled lesbians through a friendship and information network of lesbians and bisexual women of all ages. Organises socials and produces a quarterly newsletter.
C B V(Y) M(250) P

Gender Dysphoria Trust (GDT)
BM Box 7624, London WC1N 3XX
0323-641100
Contact Fran Hughes SRN
Offers help, by means of self-help - ie help from within the organisation - to those believing themselves to be transsexual. Provides a network of information and support. Offers professional counselling.
B V M(1,450) P

Genetic Clinic (Funded by Imperial Cancer Research Fund)
Royal Free Hospital, Pond Street, London NW3 2QC
Contact Dr MacDermot
Offers screening and advice to women with close relatives who have developed bowel and breast cancer before the age of 50. Please write (enclosing SAE) for appointment.

Gingerbread
35 Wellington Street, London WC2E 7BN
071-240 0953
Runs self-help groups for one-parent families throughout the UK. Provides social opportunities for adults and children, and practical advice and information.
* C B V M(8,000) S(12) P

Girl Guides Association
17-19 Buckingham Palace Road, London SW1W 0PT
071-834 6242 Fax 071-828 8317
Contact M W Hayter
Helps girls and women to contribute positively to their community and the wider world.
C B V M(8.5 million worldwide) P

Girls Alone Project (GAP)
11-12 Gosfield Street, London W1P 7HE
071-436 0388
Contact Ruby Noorani
A long-stay hostel for young single homeless women aged 16-19; provides a supportive environment in

which they can learn to take responsibility for their own lives and gain the skills necessary for independent living. Aims to rehouse women before the ir nineteenth birthday; offers resettlement support.
C B M(9) S(3)

Girls' Brigade
Girls' Brigade House, Foxhall Road, Didcot, Oxon OX11 7BQ
0235-510425 Fax 0235-510429
Contact Audrey Rowland
International, interdenominational Christian organisation. Meeting weekly, each local company aims to provide a wide range of activities to develop physical, mental and spiritual maturity. Encourages members in practical service to church, home and community; provides leadership training that is of value outside as well as within the Girls' Brigade.
* C B V M(53,396) S(26) P

Girls Friendly Society and Townsend Fellowship (GFS & TF)
Townsend House, 126 Queen's Gate, London SW7 5LQ
071-589 9628
Contact Hazel Grant Smith
World-wide Anglican society which promotes fellowship amongst girls and women and helps them to grow in the Christian faith. Works in parish-based groups, industrial mission and in shared housing. Voluntary leaders are supported by experienced staff and GFS Industrial Chaplains.
* C B M(5,000) S(32) P

Girls' Public Day School Trust
26 Queen Anne's Gate, London SW1H 9AN
071-222 9595 Fax 071-222 8771
Contact T Oakley
Aims to provide high quality academic education at relatively modest fees. Runs 26 schools with nearly 1800 girl pubils aged 5-18.
C B V P

Girls' Schools Association (GSA)
130 Regent Road, Leicester LE1 7PG 0533-541619 Fax 0533-471152
Contact Ann Parkin
Association of heads of independent girls' schools; discusses matters concerning the policy of such schools; promotes the interests of girls' education generally; fosters good codes of practice; provides a forum for exchange of views between members and other bodies engaged in education.
B V(Y) M(300) S(3) P

Girls Venture Corps Air Cadets
Redhill Aerodrome, Kingsmill Lane, South Nuffield, Redhill, Surrey RH1 5JY
0737-823345
Contact Hazel Prosper
Provides training for girls aged 12-20 to equip them for responsible citizenship, community service and an understanding of national and world affairs. Gives emphasis on Aviation Training, Duke of Edinburgh's Award Scheme and adventurous activities. Also encourages travel at home and abroad, which is arranged through the Corps.
C B V P

GLAD (Gay Legal Advice)
c/o LLGC, 69 Cowcross Street,
London EC1M 6BP
071-253 2043 (7.00-10.00pm)
Telephone advice service for legal
problems, either civil or criminal, run
by and for gay men and lesbians.
Monday-Friday 7-10 pm; lesbians
only on Wednesday. Maintains
national register of solicitors
sympathetic to gay men and lesbians.
V

Health Rights Ltd
Unit 110, BonMarche Building, 444
Brixton Road, London SW9 8EJ
071-274 4000 ext 442
Fax 071-737 5521
Contact Jane Cowl
Promotes the right of everyone to
good health care and treatment.
Carries out research, publishes
reports and booklets, organises
conferences and campaigns,
provides advice and information, on
public health and NHS issues.
V M(200) S(4) L P

**Helene Harris Memorial Trust
(HHMT)**
Harvard House, 14-16 Thames
Road, Barking, Essex IG11 0HX
081-594 5533 Fax 081-591 0962
Contact John Eric Harris
The Trust brings together
international scientists and clinicians
for 3-4 day forums biennially to
exchange information and discuss
research, detection and treatment of
ovarian cancer. The entire
proceedings are published as a
reference and teaching text book.
C V T(Harvard International Ltd) P

**Help and Advice Line for
Offenders' Wives (HALOW)**
30 Blackford Street, Winson Green,
Birmingham B18 4BN
021-523 4898
Contact Marie Curtis
Provides practical and emotional
support to the families of those in
prison either on remand or serving
sentences.
C B V(Y) M(150)

**HERA for Women (Housing
Employment Register and Advice)**
4th Floor, 2 Valentine Place, London
SE1 8QH
071-928 6141 Fax 071-401 2938
Contact Kate Hargreaves
Provides a specialist housing
employment service, with a particular
interest in women. Runs training
courses for women and a housing
employment agency via its trading
company. Provides counselling on
housing careers.
*** M(210) S(3) T(Hera Recruitment
Ltd) P**

Herpes Association
41 North Road, London N7 9DP
071-609 9061 (helpline)
071-607 9661 (admin)
Contact Michael T Wolfe
Offers advice and counselling to
people suffering from herpes
simplex. Runs telephone helpline.
Aims to inform and educate both the
public and the medical world about
HSV.
C B V M(1,000) S(2) P

Holidays One-Parents (HOP)

51 Hampshire Road, Droylsden,
Manchester M35 7PH
061-370 0337
Contact Bill Softley
Provides holidays at low cost for one-parents and their children. Disseminates information and publicity nationwide. Provides a befriending service, savings scheme, discount travel on British Rail, and information.
C V M(500) P

Housing Link for Women
8th Floor, Artillery House, Artillery Row, London SW1P 1RT
071-799 2050
Contact Julia Linfoot
Housing associations registered with the Housing Corporation providing approximately 350 flats in various locations in west and south London for single women over 40 years of age. Does not have an open waiting list, and houses council nominees and re ferrals.
C P

Hysterectomy Support Group (HSG)
The Venture, Green Lane, Upton, Huntingdon, Cambs PE17 5YE
081-690 5987
Contact Ann Webb
Provides pre- and post-operation information and informal support for women undergoing hysterectomy. Maintains a network of local contacts and some local groups.
B V M(900) P

Identity Counselling Service
Beauchamp Lodge, 2 Warwick Crescent, London W2 6NE
071-289 6175
Contact Joint Co-ordinators
Runs a counselling service to help people struggling with relationships, loss or depression, and experiencing confusion about identity or sexual orientation. Maintains a register of counsellors in the London area and in many other cities throughout England. Produces leaflets.
C B V P

Industrial Society
Robert Hyde House, 48 Bryanston Square, London W1H 7LN
071-262 2401   Fax 071-706 1096
Contact Sonia Arnold
The Pepperill Unit campaigns for greater equality of opportunity in employment. Works with organisations in the private and public sector, with individuals (women and men), and with education. Runs courses and conferences on a number of issues such a s career, personal and management development, returning to work, stress management, assertiveness and equal opportunities.
C B M(16,000) S(400) P

Infertility Advisory Centre Research Foundation
15 Berkeley Street, London W1X 5AE   071-224 4724   Fax 071-224 4725
Contact Melanie Joanne Alford
Gives advice via a hotline service at any time, about any aspect of infertility. Enables couples to have a 20-minute free consultation with a

doctor, if they are unable to afford private medicine. Gives counselling on infertility.
C B V M(1,300) S(2) T(British Association for Betterment of Infertility and Education) P

Institute for the Study of Christianity and Sexuality (ISCS)
Oxford House, Derbyshire Street, London E2 6HG
071-739 1249
Contact Secretary
Aims to advance the Christian religion by promoting objective debate within the Christian churches on matters concerning human sexuality, with a view to developing the spiritual teaching and doctrines of such churches, and by providing counselling se rvices.
C V(Y) M(300) S(1) P

International Catholic Society for Girls (ACISJF)
St Patrick's International Centre, 24 Great Chapel Street, London W1V 3AF
071-734 2156 (10am-3:15pm Mon-Thurs) Fax 071-287 6282
Contact Sheelah Clarke
Provides welfare service, advice on accommodation and job opportunities for young women travelling away from home; also au pair placements for young foreign girls in the UK and for English girls on the Continent. Offers youth club facilities and social programme.
C B V P

International Planned Parenthood Federation (IPPF)
Regent's College, Inner Circle, Regent's Park, London NW1 4LQ
071-486 0741
Contact Sunetra Puri
Initiates and supports family planning services throughout the world, and educates people and governments in the benefits for the whole family, particularly mothers and children, of spacing and planning births.
C B V M(104) S(220) P

Josephine Butler Society
49 Hawkshead Lane, North Mimms, Hatfield, Herts AL9 7TD
0707-43150
Contact Margaret Schwarz
Promotes social justice, equality of all citizens before the law and a single moral standard for men and women.
V M(200) S(1) P

Kenric
BM Kenric, London WC1N 3XX
Contact Secretary
Nationwide social organisation run for and by lesbians through network of regional representatives and contacts. Organises events and activities; offers friendship and support, particularly for geographically isolated women. Runs telephone and correspondence circle; produces monthly newsletter and diary of events.
B V M(800) P

Kids' Clubs Network (National Out of School Alliance)
279-281 Whitechapel Road, London E1 1BY
071-247 3009 Fax 071-247 4490
Contact Tess Woodcraft
Provides information, advice and development help for parents, schools, employers, etc wishing to set up after-school and holiday clubs. Produces guidelines on standards for kids' clubs. Lobbies on the need for more out-of-school care.
* C B M(500) S(9) T(The Out of School Childcare Service) P

King's Cross Women's Centre (KXWC)
71 Tonbridge Street, London WC1H 9DZ
071-837 7509
Contact Wilmette Brown
Multi-racial women's centre offers drop-in, advice and survival information on anti-racism, disability rights, immigration, welfare benefits, housing, prostitution, employment, Restart, divorce, custody, anti-lesbian discrimination, rape and violence , including racist sexual assault, etc. Several women's campaigning organisations are based at the centre. Produces a variety of publications and information packs (also available on tape).
V(Y) P

Knitting and Crochet Guild
c/o Membership Secretary, 5 Roman Mount, Roundhay, Leeds LS8 2DP
0532-664651
Contact Elizabeth Gillet
Promotes the crafts of hand and machine knitting and crochet. Participates in textile and craft exhibitions. Promotes the development of local groups interested in all three disciplines, and classes, workshops, lectures and seminars.
C B V M(1,200) P

La Leche League of Great Britain
Box BM 3424, London WC1N 3XX
071-242 1278
Contact Esther Culpin
Provides information and support to those women who want to breastfeed their babies. Offers mother-to-mother contact, local groups and publications.
C B V P

Lace Guild
The Hollies, 53 Audnam Road, Stourbridge, West Midlands DY8 4AE 0384-390739
Contact Chris Berrow
Disseminates information about lace, and about courses, classes and other events for lacemakers. Publishes patterns for lacemaking, and details of suppliers of lace requisites. Organises a touring exhibition.
C V M(8,800) S(6) T(The Lace Guild Enterprises Ltd) P L

Latin American Women's Rights Service
Albany Centre, 8 Douglas Way, Deptford, London SE8 4AG
081-694 8176
Contact Myriam Reyes
Offers advice, information and project development service to help achieve a better standard of living for Latin-American women living in the UK; covers benefits, immigration,

health, employment, education, recreation, housing, consumer and similar matters.
C V(Y) M(480) S(3) P

Law Society Women's Careers Working Party
50-52 Chancery Lane, London WC2A 1SX
071-242 1222 Fax 071-405 9522
Contact Judith McDermott
Works to develop policies promoting the interests of women solicitors.
B P

League of Jewish Women
Woburn House, Upper Woburn Place, London WC1H 0EP
071-387 7688
Contact Maureen Moses
Unites Jewish women, encouraging and stimulating them to give of themselves for the benefit of both the Jewish and wider communities, to enable them to make effective contributions to the solutions and dilemmas facing the population. Encourages the formation of local groups and co-operation with other organisations.
* C B V M(4,900) S(2) P

Legal Action for Women (LAW)
King's Cross Women's Centre, 71 Tonbridge Street, London WC1H 9DZ
071-837 7509
Contact Nina Lopez-Jones
Offers women a chance to discuss their legal cases with experienced grassroots women, offering access to sympathetic solicitors, a second legal opinion and campaigning back-up. Provides advice and support on prostitution charges, immigration, police illegality and racism, social security, child custody, divorce, rape, domestice violence, compensation, health, peace and other questions.
V

Lesbian and Gay Christian Movement (LGCM)
Oxford House, Derbyshire Street, Bethnal Green, London E2 6HG
071-739 1249 071-587 1235 (counselling helpline)
Contact General Secretary
Offers lesbian and gay liberation to the churches and Christ to the lesbian and gay community.
B V(Y) M(750) S(1) P

Lesbian and Gay Employment Rights (LAGER)
St Margaret's House, 21 Old Ford Street, London E2 4PL
081-983 0694
Fights all forms of discrimination faced by lesbians and gay men in the workplace and in agencies dealing with unemployment. Offers information, support and advice to individuals, trade unions, local authorities and voluntary agencies.
V S(4) P

Lesbian and Gay Fostering and Adoptive Parents Network
c/o London Friend, 86 Caledonian Road, London N1 9DN
Offers confidential support and contact for lesbians and gay men who are or who want to become adoptive parents or foster carers. Campaigns and distributes information.
V

Lesbian and Gay Pride Organising Committee
BM Pride, London WC1N 3XX
Contact Secretary
Organises and raises funds for annual carnival parade and festival of lesbian and gay pride.
V P

Lesbian and Gay Youth Movement (LGYM)
BM/GYM, London WC1N 3XX
081-317 9690
Offers information, advice and support for lesbians and gay men under 26 years of age, and campaigns against discrimination towards lesbians, gays and young people.
B V(Y) M(500) P

Lesbian Archive and Information Centre (LAIC)
4 Wild Court, Wesley House, London WC2B 5AV
Contact Karen
Seeks to reclaim the past and to record the present lives of lesbians on a wide and diverse scale. Maintains a library of books, photographs, postcards, press-cuttings and periodicals from Virginia Woolf to Audre Lorde.
V P

Lesbian Information Service (LIS)
PO Box 8, Todmorden, Lancs OL14 5TZ
0706-817235
Contact Sandra Lucille
Facilitates communication among lesbians and promotes understanding of lesbian experience in order to combat discrimination. Produces bi-monthly newsletter for lesbians only, occasional papers and other publications; also runs courses, groups and conducts research.
V M(150) P

Letterbox Library
1st Floor, 8 Bradbury Street, London N16 8JN
071-254 1640
Women's co-operative bookclub specialising in anti-sexist and multicultural books for children of all ages. Produces a quarterly catalogue and newsletter free to members, who are also entitled to discount on books. Services to schools are also available.
B V M(10,000+) P

LIFE (Save the Unborn Child)
LIFE House, 1a Newbold Terrace, Leamington Spa, Warwicks CV32 4EA
0926-421587 (office) 0926-311511 (helpline) Fax 0926-336497
Contact N Scarisbrick
Educates people about the nature of abortion and its consequences; helps women avoid abortion by offering free pregnancy counselling and help to any pregnant woman; campaigns in Parliament and locally for legislation which forbids all direct abortion and which offers full rights and protection to all unborn children from the moment of conception onwards. Gives talks, runs counselling offices and houses offering accomodation to pregnant women.
B V(Y) M(30,500) S(9) P

Life Care and Housing Trust
LIFE House, 1a Newbold Terrace,
Leamington Spa, Warwicks
CV32 4EA
0926-421587   Fax 0926-336497
Contact Anne Dibb
Provides free confidential help during pregnancy, after birth, after abortion. Runs 108 counselling centres and has 55 houses to accommodate homeless pregnant women and unsupported mothers and their children. Offers post-abortion trauma counselling and support; free pregnancy testing; natural fertility control and infertility counselling; also emergency placement of newborn handicapped babies.
C B V S(2) P

Lifeline - Help for Victims of Violence in the Home
6 Edward Street, Albert Village,
Burton on Trent, Staffs DE11 8ER
0283-226060
Contact Susan Dyas
Supports, advises, counsels and re-educates families experiencing abuse; works with the abuser as well as the abused person. Each family is allocated their own helper on a 24-hour, 7-day-a-week basis. Offers individual and group counselling by teleph one and correspondence.
C B V P

Local Education Authorities Equal Opportunities Consortium (LEAC)
Room 547, Institute of Education,
20 Bedford Way, London WC1H 0AL
071-636 1500 ext 762
Contact Mary Packer
Manages and supports equal opportunities initiatives in schools. Provides in-service training for teachers with responsibility for equal opportunities.
P

London Black Women's Health Action Project
c/o Bancroft Library, Bancroft Road,
London E1 4BU
081-980 3503
Contact Shamis Dirir
Promotes the good health and general well-being of black women. Campaigns against female genital mutilation; promotes research on the medical, social and psychological implications of this practice, on sexuality and mental health; produces educational material for black women, health professionals and politicians. Encourages self-help amongst black women in London.
C V P

London Friend
86 Caledonian Road, London
N1 9DN
071-837 2782
Contact Development Worker
Offers free counselling, advice and support for lesbian women and gay men. Runs regular women's support groups for lesbians, black lesbians and lesbians of colour, and for women who are coming out. Women's helpline available Tuesday and Thursday 7.30 -10 pm.
B V P

London Irish Women's Centre
59 Stoke Newington Church Street,
London N16 0AR
071-249 7318 (11am-1pm, 2-5pm Tues-Thurs)
Provides an essential service for Irish women. Offers information, welfare

advice, counselling sessions, creche and childcare facilities; acts as a focal point for Irish women's groups throughout London.
B V P

London Lesbian and Gay Centre (LLGC)
67-69 Cowcross Street, London EC1M 6BP
071-608 1471
Contact Oscar Watson
Provides a safe environment for lesbians and gay men in which they can enjoy social and support facilities. Offers meetings, discos, three bars (one for women only), restaurant, reception/information space, resident counselling project and fundraising events, etc. Over 100 groups meet at the centre each year.
V(Y) M(500) S(10)

London Lesbian and Gay Switchboard
BM Switchboard, London WC1N 3XX
071-837 7324
Contact Secretary
Twenty-four hour information and help service for lesbians and gay men. Will advise and counsel on a wide variety of issues, including AIDS/HIV, accommodation, legal problems, lesbian and gay venues and groups, coming out and sexual and social matters.
V M(120) T(Frogs Trading Ltd) P

London Lesbian Line (LLL)
Box BM 1514, London WC1N 3XX
071-251 6911 (2-10 pm Mon & Fri; 7-10 pm Tues-Thurs)
Contact Advice workers
Runs a telephone helpline; provides advice or information on local lesbian groups, social events, etc.
C V M(25) S(2) T(Women's Referral Information Service) P

London Rape Crisis Centre (LRCC)
PO Box 69, London WC1X 9NJ
071-837 1600 (counselling)
071-278 3956 (office)
Provides a free and confidential counselling service for women and girls around sexual violence. Runs a 24-hour counselling line. Offers face-to-face counselling. Provides information and public education. Undertakes research.
C V M(175) S(2) P

Low Pay Unit
9 Upper Berkeley Street, London W1H 8BY 071-262 7278
Contact Kathy Sutton
Campaigns on behalf of low-paid workers. Provides information and advice on low-paid employment rights, social security rights, trade union rights and pay; carries out research.
C M(500) T(Low Pay Unit Co Ltd) P

Marie Stopes House
The Well Woman Centre, 108 Whitfield Street, London W1P 6BE
071-388 0662
Offers help, advice, information and a medical service on all aspects of women's health, including well-woman screening, full medicals, contraception, abortion, sexual

health, female sterilisation and vasectomy for men. Low cost, short waiting time. Also offers free information and advice by telephone at certain hours. Phone the number above to find out when this service is available.
C V P

Married Women's Association
87 Redington Road, London
NW3 7RR
071-794 2884
Contact Simone Grasse
Promotes equal financial partnership in marriage and offers support to deserted wives. Campaigns on women's issues and maintains contact with MPs.
B V M(200) P

MATCH (Mothers Apart from their Children)
c/o BM Problems, London
WC1N 3XX
Contact Margaret Pearce
Offers support, friendship and understanding to any woman parted from her children through contact with others in similar circumstances. Holds informal meetings in London and the provinces, and produces a newsletter.
B V M(300) P

Maternity Alliance
15 Britannia Street, London
WC1X 9JP
071-837 1265
Contact Lyn Durward
Provides information about a wide range of maternity issues, including pre-conceptual health, employment and benefit rights. Leaflets available.
* V M(170) S(7) P

Maternity Links
The Old Co-op, 42 Chelsea Road, Easton, Bristol BS5 6AF
0272-541487
Contact Shaheen Chaudhry
Provides support, understanding, information and interpreting to pregnant non-English speaking women and their children using the health service; offers English tuition to pregnant mothers; promotes awareness of the needs of ethnic minorities amongst health professionals and voluntary workers. Video about pregnancy available in English, Urdu, Punjabi, Gujerati, Bengali, Vietnamese and Cantonese.
C V S(10) L

Maternity Services Liasion Scheme
Brady Centre, 192 Hanbury Street, London E1 5HU
071-377 8725
Community health workers accompany ethnic minority women to antenatal clinics and hospital. They carry out antenatal and post-natal care; encourage health education; advise on welfare rights and contraception. Have Bengali, Somali, Chinese and Vietna mese workers.
C

Mature Lesbian Group
c/o Camden Lesbian Centre, 54-56 Phoenix Road, London NW1 1ES
Contact Erika Nightingale
Holds monthly meetings on a Sunday afternoon; aims to provide a friendly and sympathetic atmosphere for older lesbians.
C V

Medical Women's Federation (MWF)
Tavistock House North, Tavistock Square, London WC1H 9HX
071-387 7765
Contact Hon Secretary
Considers all questions affecting the practice of medicine; promotes equal opportunities for women doctors who wish to work full or part-time; operates a careers advisory service; submits memoranda to government and other medical bodies.
C B M(2,400) S(3) P

Meet-a-Mum-Association (MAMA)
c/o 58 Malden Avenue, London SE25 4HS
081-656 7318
Contact Briony Hallam
Self-help organisation for all new mothers and those with young children who may feel tired, lonely, isolated and/or depressed after the birth of a child.
C B V M(2,000) S(1)

Microsyster
Wesley House, 4 Wild Court, Off Kingsway, London WC2B 5AU
071-430 0655
Feminist computer collective which offers services to women's groups in London including computer consultancy, training and support, and statistical analysis for surveys. Also provides access to computers for groups to maintain their own subs/mailing lists. Runs women's mailing list; produces a newsletter and publications.
V M(6) P

Midwives Information and Resource Service (MIDIRS)
Institute of Child Health, Royal Hospital for Sick Children, St Michael's Hill, Bristol BS2 8BJ
0272-251791
Contact Joy Rodwell
Provides up-to-date information to midwives and other childbirth professionals on all aspects of maternity care.
* C V M(4,750) S(7) P

Milton Keynes Women and Work Group
6 Church Street, Wolverton, Milton Keynes, Bucks MK12 5JN
0908-310372
Contact Jenny Charlwood
Promotes job and training opportunities for women. Offers advice; runs courses on returning to work; produces publications on jobs, training and childcare.
V S(3) P

Miscarriage Association
PO Box 24, Ossett, West Yorks WF5 9XG
0924-830515
Contact Kathryn Ladley
Provides information and support for women and their families during and after miscarriage.
C B V M(900) P

Money Management Council
18 Doughty Street, London WC1N 2PL 071-405 1985
Contact John Moysey
Promotes better understanding, improved general education and increased self-help in personal and family money management.
* C L P

Mothers' Union
Mary Sumner House, 24 Tufton
Street, London SW1P 3RB
071-222 5533
Contact Margaret Chapman
Worldwide organisation concerned
with all matters that strengthen and
preserve marriage and Christian
family life. Works with families in the
UK and abroad.
*** C B V P**

**Movement for the Ordination of
Women (MOW)**
Napier Hall, Hide Place, Vincent
Street, London SW1P 4NJ
071-834 2736 Fax 071-834 7238
Contact Caroline Davis
Aims to promote the ordination of
women to the priesthood in the
Church of England as a fundamental
part of the ministry of men and
women.
B V M(4,000) S(3) P

Multiple Births Foundation (MBFI)
Queen Charlotte's and Chelsea
Hospital, Goldhawk Road, London
W6 0XG
081-748 4666
Contact Dr Elizabeth Bryan MD
FRCP
Gives professional support to
families with twins, triplets, etc.
Educates professionals and the
public on the needs of multiple birth
families. Provides an advisory
service to parents and professionals,
and a media resource centre for
research workers.
C V M(250) S(7) P

National Abortion Campaign
Wesley House, 4 Wild Court, London
WC2B 5AU
071-405 4801
Contact Leonora Lloyd
Aims to defend and extend women's
abortion rights. Campaigns against
attacks on abortion; produces
educational and other material, and
AIDS/HIV educational material.
B V(Y) M(600) S(2) P

**National Alliance for Women of
African Descent**
Women's Centre, 603 High Road,
Leyton, London E10 6RF
081-556 4053
Contact Veronica Roach
Provides a forum and staffed centre
for women of African descent.
Disseminates information to member
organisations on the ways in which
they can organise around issues for
their general advancement.
C B V P

**National Alliance of Women's
Organisations (NAWO)**
279-281 Whitechapel Road, London
E1 1BY
071-247 7052
Contact Jane Grant
Umbrella organisation acting as
advocate and support for all women's
groups with headquarters in England;
has more than 185 member
organisations representing around 5
million women. Maintains strong links
with similar alliances in Scotland,
Northern Ireland and Wales, and is
involved in the setting up of the
European Women's Lobby.
* C V(Y) M(185) L S(3) P

National Association for Maternal and Child Welfare
1 South Audley Street, London
W1Y 6JS
071-493 2601
Contact William Hedley
Promotes education in human development, childcare and family life. Syllabuses available on request. Publishes a variety of leaflets and arranges study days.
* C B V M(100) S(5) T(Comatchwel Ltd) P

National Association for Premenstrual Syndrome (NAPS)
PO Box 72, Sevenoaks, Kent
TN13 1QX
0732-459378 0227-763133 (helpline)
Self-help group for sufferers from pre-menstrual syndrome and post-natal depression. Offers advice and information, also local contacts.
C B V(Y) M(1,215) S(1) P

National Association for the Childless
Birmingham Settlement, 318 Summer Lane, Birmingham B19 3RL
021-359 4887 Fax 021-359 6357
Contact Jill Dorrell
Helps those who are struggling to have children. Gives advice about fertility problems; listens to feelings and worries during treatment; and helps people to cope if all else fails.
C B V T(The Childless Trust) P

National Association of Citizens Advice Bureaux (NACAB)
115-123 Pentonville Road, London
N1 9LZ
071-833 2181 Fax 071-833 4371
Contact Jacqui Roach
Provides free confidential and impartial service of information and advice on all subjects through 1230 outlets nationwide. Communicates experience of clients' problems to policy makers.
* C B V P

National Association of Ladies' Circles of Great Britain and Ireland (NALC)
Provincial House, Cooke Street, Keighley, West Yorks BD21 3NN
0535-607617 Fax 0535-662312
Contact Marlene Sharkey
Friendship and service organisation involved with service in the community and fundraising activities. Organises meetings, social functions and outings.
B V M(12,000) S(4) T(NALC Sales Dept) P

National Association of Local Government Women's Committees
The Pankhurst Centre, 60/62 Nelson Street, Chorlton-on-Medlock, Manchester M13 9WP
061-274 3684
Contact Marilyn Taylor
Provides a forum for information exchange and support. Considers initiatives local councils could take up in relation to the needs of women; shares ideas of good policy and practice; monitors the development of initiatives of women's committees.

The association meets over two days four times a year.
B

National Association of Natural Family Planning Teachers (NANFPT)
NFP Centre, Birmingham Maternity Hospital, Queen Elizabeth Centre, Edgbaston, Birmingham B15 2GT
051-526 7663 Fax 021-472 0061
Contact Wyn Worthington
Co-ordinates the activities of certified NFP teachers and promotes high standards of training and practice. Stimulates and assists in NFP teacher training programmes in all areas, and facilitates the exchange of information and updating on all matters of fertility and NFP practice and research.
C B V M(300) P

National Association of Widows/Widows Advisory Trust
54-57 Allison Street, Digbeth, Birmingham B5 5TH
021-643 8348
Contact Lynne Davies
Offers advice, information and friendly support to all widows and their families. Branches throughout the country provide the basis of a supportive social life, while head office provides free, specialist advice and information.
* C B V M(3,500) S(3) P

National Association of Women Pharmacists (NAWP)
40 Norwood Thornhill, Cardiff CF4 9DE
0222-521336
Contact Peggy Baker
Represents women within pharmacy and women pharmacists in other organisations. Holds an annual weekend school and one-day courses to encourage continuing education and career development for women pharmacists.
B V(Y) M(400) P

National Association of Women's Clubs
5 Vernon Rise, King's Cross Road, London WC1X 9EP
071-837 1434
Contact Stella Nicholas
Provides facilities for informal education for women over the age of 18. Through an interest in new skills and activities aims to stimulate confidence and a sense of responsibility which can be extended into the local community.
* C B V M(14,000)

National Board of Catholic Women (NBCW)
83 Alleyn Road, London SE21 8AD
081-670 7919
Contact Anne Leeming
Forms a consultative body to the Bishops' Conference of England and Wales, consisting of representatives from 20 Catholic organisations. Explores and expresses the opinions of Catholic women and keeps a watchful eye on legislation affecting women and the family.
P

National British Women's Total Abstinence Union
23 Dawson Place, London W2 4TH
071-229 0804
Contact Secretary
Works to promote total abstinence from alcohol by education and other means; provides information on the dangers of alcohol; works for peace, human rights and moral parity.
C B V P

National Campaign for Nursery Education (NCNE)
23 Albert Street, London NW1 7LU
071-387 6582 Fax 071-387 6582
Contact Valerie Kotzen
Promotes the provision of quality nursery education for every child under five. Campaigns for statutory but not mandatory nursery education, and for a qualified teacher, specially trained in nursery education, in charge of every class.
B V M(250,000) P

National Childbirth Trust (NCT)
Alexandra House, Oldham Terrace, London W3 6NH
081-992 8637 Fax 081-992 5929
Contact Mary Newburn
Educates parents for pregnancy, birth and early parenthood. Runs antenatal classes, breastfeeding counselling, postnatal support in branches throughout the UK, support for disabled parents, and parenthood education in schools.
* C B V M(48,716) S(25) T(NCT Maternity Sales Ltd) L P

National Childminding Association
8 Masons Hill, Bromley, Kent
BR2 9EY
081-464 6164 Fax 081-290 6834
Contact Sue Owen
Promotes the status of childminding through mutual self-help groups, information, advice and training. The association has 40,000 members comprising childminders, parents and local authority workers.
* C B V M(40,000) S(2) T(Childminding in Business) P

National Citizen Advocacy
2 St Paul's Road, London N1 2QR
071-359 8289
Contact Sally Carr Resource and advisory centre for anyone involved in citizen advocacy. Offers independent, voluntary representation to people who are unable themselves to defend or exercise their rights.
C B V(Y) S(1) P

National Council for Abducted Children (RE-UNITE)
PO Box 4, London WC1X 8XY
071-404 8356
Contact Lucy Jaffe
Provides advice, support and information to parents (usually mothers, since the majority of abducters are men) of children who have been forcibly taken overseas as a result of relationship breakdown or divorce. Also advises professionals working on a bduction cases, and maintains contact with relevant government departments and voluntary agencies throughout the world.
B V M(100) S(1) P

National Council for Civil Liberties (Liberty)
21 Tabard Street, London SE1 4LA
071-403 3888 Fax 071-407 5354
Contact Jane Sill
Current work of the Women's Rights Unit includes campaigning for improvements to the existing sex discrimination and equal pay laws; advising employers and trade unions on positive action programmes to introduce genuine equal opportunities in the workplace; helping women combat sexual and racial harassment at work; fighting important cases to determine how far the existing legislation can help women.
* B V M(8,000) S(17) P

National Council for One Parent Families (NCOPF)
255 Kentish Town Road, London NW5 2LX
071-267 1361 Fax 071-482 4851
Contact Head of Information Department
Provides advice and information on benefits, housing, employment, family law, etc. for one-parent families and those who work with them. Campaigns to improve provisions for all single-parent families. Produces a wide range of publications.
* C M(600) S(20) P

National Council for the Divorced and Separated
13 High Street, Little Shelford, Cambridge CB2 5ES
0533-708880
Over 100 branches nationwide provide social actities and welfare advice and guidance for all divorced and separated people; access to national and regional welfare officers.
C B V P

National Council of Women of Great Britain
36 Danbury Street, London N1 8JU
071-354 2395
Membership of NCW is open to all women who wish to participate in the life of Great Britain. Holds regular meetings at branches throughout England, Scotland and Wales to debate and study the issues of the day. Works in conjunction with 86 affiliated national organisations.
* C B V P

National Debtline
Birmingham Settlement, 318 Summer Lane, Birmingham B19 3RL
021-359 8501 Fax 021-359 6357
Contact Jeff Brown
Runs a telephone helpline to provide basic advice for people in debt about their options and their legal rights, and offers information to other workers who may lack specialist support. Issues callers with a self-help information pack.
S(4) P

National Family Conciliation Council
Shaftesbury Centre, Percy Street, Swindon, Wilts SN2 2AZ
0793-514055 Fax 0793-512477
Contact Thelma Fisher
Fosters the provision of independent family conciliation services, and supports those services already in existence.
M(35) S(1) P

National Federation of Community Organisations (NFCO)
8-9 Upper Street, London N1 0PQ
071-226 0189
Contact Diana Hopkins
Promotes the activities of local community organisations in the areas of education, recreation and social welfare. Provides support for training, information, advice, publications and practical help; promotes local networks, and represents the interests of its members nationally.
* C B V M(1,067) S(18) T P

National Federation of Self-Help Organisations
150 Townmead Road, London SW6 2RA
071-731 8440
Contact Dr Vince Hines
Acts as the main co-ordinating body for self-help organisations, serving the whole of the UK. Membership is available to groups committed to community development in a wide variety of fields, including community and youth work, education, housing, health, co-operative activities and the arts.
B V M(2,500 groups) P

National Federation of Women's Institutes
104 New Kings Road, London SW6 4LY 071-371 9300 Fax 071-736 3652
Contact General Secretary
Largest women's organisation in the UK, which offers activities in sport, the arts, public affairs, crafts, international understanding, the environment, etc. Owns short-stay adult education college in Oxfordshire and publishing company.

Organises weekly co-operative markets nationwide.
* C B V(Y) M(347,000 approx) S(75) T(WI Books Ltd) P

National Free Church Women's Council
27 Tavistock Square, London WC1H 9HH
071-387 8413 Fax 071-383 0150
Contact Pauline Butcher
Undertakes voluntary service for the relief and support of those in need. In conjunction with local Free Church Women's Councils in many parts of the country: provides homes and flatlets for elderly people; a home and hostel for girls needing special care; hospital visitation and Free Church services.
C B V

National Friend (FRIEND)
BM Friend, London WC1N 3XX
Contact Norma Thompson
Provides information, advice, support, befriending and counselling to gay, lesbian and bisexual people, and their associates.
C B V M(364) P

National Homeworking Unit
3rd Floor, Wolverley House, 18 Digbeth, Birmingham B5 6BJ
021-643 6352
Contact Administration and Information Officer
Advocates the rights of homeworkers in order to better their conditions of employment; campaigns for equal opportunities for homeworkers in education, training, childcare and employment. Areas of work cover education, training and employment;

health and safety; lobbying and legislative change; and information.
P

National Housewives Association (NHA)
Flat 4, 68 Somerset Place, Stoke, Plymouth, Devon PL1 3QP
0752-20457
Contact Gloria Ford
Puts forward the views and opinions of housewives to MPs, Euro-MPs, manufacturers, producers, government departments and others on such issues as women returning to work after childbearing, child benefit, widows, education, retirement, housing, food supplies, environment issues, factory farming, legal aid and television standards.
V P

National Information for Parents of Prematures: Education, Resources and Support (NIPPERS)
c/o The Sam Segal Perinatal Unit, St Mary's Hospital, Praed Street, London W2 1NY
Contact Caroline Kerr-Smith
Encourages the setting up of support groups; helps parents make contact with other parents of prematures; writes information leaflets; organises events, conferences and workshops; answers queries from parents; conducts a survey of support available for parents, and into levels of staff stress.
C B V M(150) P

National Joint Committee of Working Women's Organisations
150 Walworth Road, London SE17 1JT
071-703 0833
Contact Vicky Phillips
Promotes the interests of working women and assists in securing their representation on any local, national or international committees, or similar bodies established by government or other authorities to deal with matters in which women have a special interest.
*

National Organisation for Women's Management Education (NOWME)
132 Abbey Road, London NW6 6SN
071-624 6260
Contact Dorothy Badrick
Provides a resource service/information centre for those interested in women's career progression and acts as a national network for members.
* M(250) P

National Osteoporosis Society
Barton Meade House, PO Box 10, Radstock, Bath, Avon BA3 3YB
0761-32472
Contact Vanessa Collier
Aims to relieve sickness and to promote and advance medical knowledge, especially concerning osteoporosis and similar and related conditions. Undertakes research and publishes results. Helps sufferers by letter and phone, newsletters and local groups .
C B V(Y) M(10,000) S(10) P

National Rett Syndrome Association (NRSA)
15 Tanzieknowe Drive, Cambuslang, Glasgow G72 8RG
041-641 7662
Contact Isobel Allen
Promotes awareness of Rett Syndrome; puts parents in touch with each other; supports parents, carers and families of girls suffering from Rett Syndrome. Offers information and advice.
C V M(220) P

National Rubella Council
Bray Business Centre, Weir Bank, Monkey Island Lane,
Bray-on-Thames, Berks SL6 2ED
0628-770011 Fax 0628-770701
Contact Julia Lindley-French
Gives advice and information about rubella immunisation. Promotes rubella campaign and aims to increase public awareness of rubella immunisation.
C B V S(3) P

National Self-Help Support Networks
c/o NCVO, 26 Bedford Square, London WC1B 3HU
071-636 4066 Fax 071-436 3188
Contact Jean Harding
Supports three national networks for self-help support workers: a network for local workers; a network for black workers; and a network for specialist organisations. They all act primarily as informal support systems for the workers. Each network meets once a year to share information, strengthen links and break the isolation of people involved in self-help support.
P

National Society for the Prevention of Cruelty to Children (NSPCC)
67 Saffron Hill, London EC1N 8RS
071-242 1626
Contact Lynne Stockbridge
Aims to prevent child abuse in all its forms. Provides 24-hour, 7-day-a-week service to children and families. Maintains network of Child Protection Teams throughout the UK. The Child Protection Teams offer skilled treatment to families and professional advice and consultation to other agencies. Daycare services include playgroups, family care and drop-in centres.
* V(Y) S(1,500) P

National Women's Network for International Solidarity (NWN)
Box 110, 190 Upper Street, London N1 1RQ
Contact Mandy Macdonald
Runs a network among British women and women from other countries living in the UK around international issues affecting women. Links women's struggles worldwide through information exchange and feminist solidarity. Publishes monthly newsletter and m aintains register of members to facilitate networking; member of National Alliance of Women's Organisations (NAWO) and Women in Development Europe (WIDE).
V M(150) S(1) P

National Women's Register
9 Bank Plain, Norwich, Norfolk
NR2 4SL
0603-765392
Contact Lesley Appel
Offers all women the opportunity to take part in informal discussion of a wide range of non-domestic topics both serious and light-hearted, and enables them to find friends quickly when moving to a new area. Local groups meet in members' homes to research subjects of mutual interest.
* C B V(Y) M(18,000) S(1) P

NATO Alerts Network
58 Coolhurst Road, London N8 8EU
081-348 6269
Contact Shirley Laird
Network of parliamentarians, researchers and others throughout the NATO alliance providing prompt, accurate information concerning NATO decisions. Encourages and assists women parliamentarians to take part in defence debates and to suggest alternatives to a defence relying heavily on military solutions to international conflict. Disseminates material produced by the Oxford Research Group or by Brussels office.
B V

Network for Supporting Children of People with Mental Distress (NSCPMD)
40 Birch House, Tulse Hill, London SW2 2ET
081-671 5084
Contact Alison McFadden
Puts adult children of mentally distressed people in touch with each other. Provides a safe atmosphere in which to discuss issues, feelings and troubles. Gives support by telephone, post and personal contact. Provides information on where to find help.
B M(50) P

New Ways to Work (NWW)
309 Upper Street, London N1 2TY
071-226 4026
Contact Charles Monkcom
Advances knowledge about all aspects of flexible work patterns through education and research. Promotes new approaches to the time patterns of work, in order to encourage equal access to jobs for people who have caring and domestic responsibilities for people with disabilities.
* C V M(200) S(4) P

Northern Concord
PO Box 258, Manchester M60 1LN
A self-help group for transvestites and transsexuals offering advice and information. Offers support to wives and girlfriends of transvestites/transsexuals. Runs a Women's Helpline.
P

Older Feminist Network
c/o 54 Gordon Road, London N3 1EP
081-346 1900
Contact Astra Blaug
Set up in response to the feeling that the larger women's liberation movement did not sufficiently recognise the problems of older women. Hopes, fears and ambitions are shared in monthly meetings and regular newsletters; through mutual support endeavours to become a more significant influence on society.
B P

One Plus One, Marriage and Partnership Research
Central Middlesex Hospital, Acton Lane, London NW10 7NS
081-965 2367 Fax 081-965 2396
Contact Susan Adams
Aims to build through research a foundation of understanding about contemporary marriage and partnership and put these findings into practice in order to prevent family breakdown. Undertakes original research; provides counselling and therapy service, education and training; acts as an information resource.
C S(9) L P

One-Parent Family Holidays (OPF Holidays)
Kildonan Courtyard, Barr Hill, Girvan, South Ayrshire KA26 0PS
0465-82288
Contact Colin Chatfield
Organises holidays for one-parent families in the UK and abroad. They book the holidays and generally act as a guiding hand.
V P

One-Parent Housing
115 Park Street, London W1Y 4DY
081-450 4629
Runs three hostels, with wardens, for single mothers and babies up to two years old.
C

Open Door Association
c/o 447 Pensby Road, Heswall, Wirral, Merseyside L61 9PQ
Runs information service for people suffering from anxiety agoraphobia, and related conditions.
V P

Open University Women into Science and Engineering (WISE) Group
Open University, Walton Hall, Milton Keynes, Bucks MK7 6AA
0908-652412 Fax 0908-653744
Encourages women to study courses in science, mathematics and technology; offers support to women students and staff in these areas. Raises awareness among all students and teaching staff about equal opportunity needs for women.
V P

Ormiston Trust
10 Abercorn Place, London NW8 9XP
071-289 8166
Contact P G Murray
Funds projects for children under 12 at risk and their families.
* C B V(Y) S(10) T(Ormiston Trust Ltd)

Over Forty Association for Women Workers
Mary George House, 120-122 Cromwell Road, London SW7 4ET
071-370 2556
Contact Kate Hargreaves
Provides housing accomodation for working women of limited income who are over 40 years of age and on their own in London; offers advice on employment.
C M(25) S(13) P

Overeaters Anonymous
PO Box 19, Stretford, Manchester M32 9EB
Offers a practical programme towards recovery for people with eating disorders, which incorporates

fellowship, regular meetings and mutual self-help.
B P

PACE (Project for Advice, Counselling and Information)
c/o 67/69 Cowcross Street, London EC1M 6BP
071-251 2689
Contact Mary Lynne Ellis
Provides counselling and art therapy to individuals, couples and groups by and for lesbians and gay men; also training in counselling, HIV/AIDS issues and heterosexism awareness.
C V

Pankhurst Trust
The Pankhurst Centre, 60-62 Nelson Street, Chorlton on Medlock, Manchester M13 9WP
061-273 5673
Contact Rachelle Warburton
Has raised funds to save and restore Emmeline Pankhurst's house in Manchester and convert the buildings into a centre which commemorates the suffrage movement and also provides a range of resources for women.
C V(Y) M(380) S(4) T(Pankhurst Press) P

Parent Network
44-46 Caversham Road, London NW5 2DS
071-485 8535 Fax 071-267 4426
Contact Ginny Dodd
Offers support groups (known as Parent-Link) to enable parents to talk about the day-to-day ups and downs of family life, and to learn new ways of handling old situations. Groups available nationwide.
* C B V S(8) P

Parents Against INjustice (PAIN)
Conifers, 2 Pledgdon Green, Nr Henham, Bishop's Stortford, Herts CM22 6BN
0279-850545 Fax 0279-850545
Contact Sue Amphlett
Offers advice and support to parents and other carers who are mistakenly suspected of child abuse or neglect. Advances public knowledge of child care laws and procedures; supports children involved in such cases; promotes family life; encourages research and publication of the results.
* C B V M(4,000) S(5) P

Parents Anonymous
Manor Gardens Centre, 6-9 Manor Gardens, London N7 6LA
071-263 8918
Contact Sally Sturgeon
Provides a helpline and listening service for parents under stress.
C B V P

Parents with Disabilities Group (of the National Childbirth Trust)
Alexandra House, Oldham Terrace, London W3 6NH
081-992 8637
Contact Jo O'Farrell
Maintains national contact register of parents with disabilities willing to offer help and support to other parents. Provides resource list on pregnancy, birth and early parenthood; offers practical tips and information on aids, equipment and support . Gives talks; helps at workshops, conferences, etc.
C B V P

Partners Group for Partners and Families of Transsexuals (Partners Group)
BM Box 6093, London WC1N 3XX
0323-641100
Contact Fran Hughes SRN
Provides a support network and a focus of understanding for those whose partner or a member of their family is transsexual. Provides confidential help via correspondence. Puts people in contact with others who are in similar situations.
V P

Pascal Theatre Company
149 Cavendish Mansions,
Clerkenwell Road, London
EC1R 5EQ
071-837 5390 Fax 071-608 2620
Contact Julia Pascal
Produces new stage plays and occasionally neglected classics; priority is given to women's writing.
C V

Peace House
Old Manse, Greenloaning, by Dunblane, Perthshire FK15 0NB
0786-88490
Contact Ellen Moxley
Small centre for conferences studying issues of peace and justice; the aim is that people should leave Peace House with refreshed spirits, heightened energy, and renewed commitment to action. Offers courses and training and educational facilities, or groups may book in their own courses; the programme has included 'Women and Anger' and 'Mothers and Daughters', led by a clinical psychiatrist. The centre can sleep six or provide for 20 on a day basis.
C V P

Phobics Society
4 Cheltenham Road,
Chorlton-cum-Hardy, Manchester
M21 1QN
061-881 1937
Contact Harold Fisher
Offers information, advice and counselling to people with phobias, depression and obsessional neurosis. Where possible, arranges help when the conditions prove incapacitating.
C B V P

Portia Trust (Future Friends)
Maryport Workspace, Salway Trading Estate, Maryport, Cumbria CA15 8NF 0900-812114 (day) 0900-812379 (evenings)
Contact Ken Norman
Produces a monthly magazine to help lonely, depressed or disadvantaged people find friends or marriage partners. Provides assistance for people facing shoplifting or similar charges. Offers help to women who have snatched, or might snatch, babies.
C B V(Y) M(12,000) S(6) P

Positively Women (PW)
5 Sebastian Street, London
EC1V 0HE
071-490 5515 Fax 071-490 1690
Contact Fiona MacGillivray
Provides care and support for women with HIV infection, AIDS or associated conditions. Services include weekly support groups, one-to-one and telephone

counselling, education and information.
C V S(7) T(Positively Prophets) P

Practical Alternatives for Mums, Dads and Under-Fives (PRAM)
c/o 162 Holland Road, Hurst Green, Oxted, Surrey RH8 9BQ
Contact Chrissie Denham
Aims to promote and improve facilities for parents who have children under five. Compiles, produces and distributes a directory of information; plans further initiatives to assist parents of young children. Distributes a newsletter to members, and provides them with information.
C V P

Pre-Eclamptic Toxaemia Society (PETS)
Eaton Lodge, 8 Southend Road, Hockley, Essex SS5 4QQ
0702-205088
Contact Sharon Copping
Acts as a support and self-help group for fellow sufferers and professionals and for lay groups interested in this condition.
C B V M(500) P

Pre-School Playgroups Association
61-63 Kings Cross Road, London WC1X 9LL
071-833 0991 Fax 071-837 4942
Contact Margaret Lochrie
Encourages the formation of playgroups and parent and toddler groups for children under five and the active involvement of parents in providing them.
*C B V

Pregnancy Advisory Service
13 Charlotte Street, London W1P 1HD
071-637 8962 Fax 071-323 4215
Contact Tara Kaufmann
Provides counselling and a referral service for women with unwanted pregnancies; pregnancy testing; post-coital contraception; sterilisation; donor insemination. Also offers training, information, public speaking and financial assistance.
* C B M(170) S(150)

Premenstrual Society (PREMSOC)
PO Box 102, London SE1 7ES
Contact
Michael Brush Gives information and support to individual sufferers from Premenstrual Syndrome (PMS) and their families. Provides specialised individual advice on PMS matters both to members and the public. Runs educational courses on PMS for professionals. Helps individuals and organisations to start local groups, clinics, etc.
B V M(450) P

Prisoners Advice and Information Network (PAIN)
BM Pain, London WC1N 3XX
081-542 3744 Maintains an information and advice network linking the following organisations: Black Female Prisoners Scheme; Women in Prison; PROP - the National Prisoners Movement; INQUEST -Deaths in Custody; Radical Alternatives to Prison. Answers enquiries and makes referrals from prisoners or their families regarding all aspects of their

treatment as prisoners, or as prisoners' families.

Prisoners Families and Friends Service (PF & FS)
51 Borough High Street, London SE1 1NB 071-403 4091
Contact Jenny Radford
Assists the families and friends of people in prison with any of the immediate problems which arise as a result of imprisonment; provides information and advice to the families of prisoners on any matter resulting from imprisonment; offers friendship and support to families and friends of prisoners during the period of imprisonment.
C V M(100) S(3)

Prisoners Wives and Families Society
254 Caledonian Road, London N1 0NG
071-278 3981
Contact Pauline Hoare
Assists prisoners' families and friends with advice and counselling; runs a small family hostel; provides holiday accomodation; offers free legal advice.
C V S(2) P

Pro-Choice Alliance (PCA)
54 Grange Road, Lewes, East Sussex BN7 1TU
0273-471814
Contact Jane Roe
National umbrella group of organisations and individuals that campaigns for a more liberal abortion law; for easier access for women to free abortion services; and for women to be able to choose for themselves whether or not to continue with an unplanned pregnancy.
V(Y) M(524) P

PROGRESS (Campaign for Research into Human Reproduction)
27-35 Mortimer Street, London W1N 7RJ
071-436 4528 Fax 071-436 3288
Contact Denise Servante
Supports and protects controlled research into the earliest stages of human development and the prevention of infertility, miscarriage and congenital handicap. Encourages a wider exchange of discussion between the public, scientists and parliamentarians. Fights any legislation or controls which seek to ban research on the human pre-embryo (a fertilised egg up to 14 days of development).
S(1)

Queen's Nursing Institute
3 Albemarle Way, London EC1V 4JB
071-490 4227
Contact Sarah Andrews
Works closely with the district health authorities to provide information and advice on all aspects of community nursing care. Provides financial assistance to sick and retired nurses, with priority being given to district nurses. Grants are also made to institutions and individuals for educational purposes.
C S(7)

Quilters' Guild
OP66 Dean CLough Business Park,
Halifax HX3 5AX
0422-345631
Contact The Administrator
Promotes the greater understanding, appreciation and knowledge of the art, techniques and heritage of patchwork, applique and quilting; encourages and maintains the highest standards of design and workmanship in both traditional and contemporary styles of work.
C M(5,600+)

Radclyffe Hall Memorial Fund
Ham Green Cottage, Wittersham,
Kent TN30 7EG
0797-270745
Contact Monica Still
Aims to restore the vault in Highgate Cemetery of Radclyffe Hall, author of 'The Well of Loneliness'.
V P

Reading Women's Education Project Ltd
c/o Ashmead School,
Northumberland Avenue, Reading
RG2 8DJ
0734-756255
Contact Penny Hiron
Provides vocational training in woodworking skills, painting and decorating for women who are under-represented in the construction industry.
V

Redwood Women's Training Association
Invergarry, Kitlings Lane, Walton on the Hill, Stafford ST17 0LE
0785-662823
Contact Maggie Mitchell
Maintains a network of trained assertiveness facilitators throughout Britain and Eire. Provides courses in assertiveness training and sexuality for both personal and professional development enabling women and men to grow in confidence, self-assurance and effectiveness.
B M(110) S(1) P

Relate: National Marriage Guidance
Herbert Gray College, Little Church Street, Rugby, Warwicks CV21 3AP
0788-73241 Fax 0788-535007
Co-ordinates the activities of local Relate (marriage guidance) centres which undertake education in personal relationships, and counselling for people seeking help in marriage and family relationships and sexual problems.
* C B V S(75) P

Rights of Women
52-54 Featherstone Street, London
EC1Y 8RT
071-251 6577 Fax 071-608 0928
Contact Linda Bean
Conducts research and disseminates information about new and existing legislation as it affects women by organising conferences, providing speakers and producing publications on aspects of the law concerning women. Offers advice and assistance on legal problems, and acts as a referral agency. Provides a forum for training, discussions and

mutual support for women working in the legal profession.
V M(250) S(6) P

Roman Catholic Feminists (RCF)
c/o 33 Arlow Road, London N21 3JS
081-886 0779
Unites and supports Roman Catholic feminists in their efforts to integrate feminism and Roman Catholicism.
B M(300) P

Royal British Legion Women's Section
48 Pall Mall, London SW1Y 5JY
071-930 8131   Fax 071-839 7917
Contact National Secretary
Promotes the welfare of ex-servicewomen, and wives and widows of ex-servicemen who may be in financial need. Weekly allowances, periods of rest and convalescence, and financial grants may be given.
 C B V M(130,000) S(17)

Royal College of Midwives Trust
15 Mansfield Street, London
W1M 0BE
071-580 6523   Fax 071-436 3951
Contact Professional Officer
Professional organisation exclusively for midwives. Speaks on all matters related to mothers and babies and the maternity services; deals with government departments and other organisations in promoting the art and science of midwifery and the optimum care of mothers and babies in the pre-and post-natal periods and during the birth process.
C B P

Royal College of Nursing
20 Cavendish Square, London
W1M 0AB
071-409 3333   Fax 071-408 0190
Professional trade union and post-certificated body for nurses; membership open to nurses on, or training for, the UKCC Register. The majority of the 285,000 members are women. Regional offices in every health region in England, plus offices in Scotl and, Ireland and Wales.
B V M(285,000) P

Royal School of Needlework (RSN)
Apartment 38, Hampton Court Palace, East Molesey, Surrey
KT8 9AU
081-943 1432
Contact Elizabeth Elvin
Promotes the art of needlework, and maintains, by teaching and example, the use of traditional stitches in ornamental embroidery and needlework; creates designs for specially-commissioned works, and offers a large choice of materials and equipment for all kinds of embroidery. Runs day and evening classes in most styles of embroidery.
C B V(Y) M(1,800) S(68) P

Salvation Army Investigation Department
105-109 Judd Street, London
WC1H 9TS
071-387 2772
Contact Major Colin Fairclough
Works for the restoration of family relationships through tracing missing relatives.
C

Samaritans
17 Uxbridge Road, Slough, Berks
SL1 1SN
0753-32713 Fax 0753-24322
Contact Simon Armson
Offers a 24-hour, widely publicised, absolutely confidential service for people who are in despair, many of whom feel suicidal.
* C B V M(22,500) S(12)

Sangam Association for Asian Women
235-237 West Hendon Broadway, London NW9 7DH
081-202 4629
Contact J Kamath
Runs classes in Hindi, Gujrati and classical Indian dance for children, sewing and other classes for women, a senior citizens' luncheon and social club, and a library and advice centre offering general advice on housing, welfare rights, etc to the Asian community.
C V P

Schoolmistresses and Governesses Benevolent Institution
SGBI Office, Queen Mary House, Manor Park Road, Chislehurst, Kent BR7 5PY
081-468 7997
Contact Richard Hayward
Offers help to women who have worked in all facets of education, including administration, and who find themselves in straitened circumstances or in a position of temporary need. Provides advice, support and financial assistance to enable them to enjoy life and receive proper care and attention; comfort and security are a concern as well as needs. Runs a residential home.
C P

Scout and Guide Graduate Association (SAGGA)
31 Baden Road, Guildford, Surrey GU2 6NZ
0483-579436
Contact Elizabeth Brown
Provides a pool of professional people with experience of the Scout and Guide movement who are ready to assist with projects connected with the movement. Holds an annual national conference, an annual summer camp. and other meetings throughout the ye ar; runs study/discussion sessions and workshops; organises camps, practical sessions and social events.
C B M(200) P

Sex, Race and Class (Black and Third World Women's Discussion and Study Group) (SRC)
King's Cross Women's Centre, 71 Tonbridge Street, London WC1H 9DZ 071-837 7509
Contact Sara Callaway
Aims to break down divisions between Asian, African, Latin-American, Afro-Carribean and other black and Third world women of different ages, abilities and disabilities, sexual choices and lifestyles.
P

Shadow Ministry for Women
PO Box 1101, London SW1A 2HY
071-219 5028 Fax 071-219 6693
Contact Jo Richardson
Aims to publicise and promote the proposal for a Ministry of Women to

be established; to encourage research and publicity; and to develop an action plan for the Ministry when it is in place.
V P

Singapore and Malaysia British Association (Women's Section) (SIMBA)
37 Handforth Road, London
SW9 0LL
071-582 3261
Contact Lucia
Human rights group supporting women's struggle in Malaysia and Singapore. Provides educational activities in the UK.
V P

Society for Advancement of Research into Anorexia (SARA)
Stanthorpe, New Pound, Wisborough Green, West Sussex RH14 0EJ
0403-700210
Contact J M Jones
Aims to promote and sponsor research into anorexia nervosa, and to further understanding of the disorder.
C B V P

Society for the Protection of Unborn Children
7 Tufton Street, London SW1P 3QN
071-222 5845 Fax 071-222 0630
Contact John Smeaton
Campaigns for legislation to protect unborn children; organises political and educational campaigns; arranges public meetings and educational projects; provides advice and information on pro-life matters.
B V(Y) T(SPUC Merchandising Division) P

Society of Women Writers and Journalists
1 Oakwood Park Road, London
N14 6QB
081-886 2436
Contact Hon Secretary
Society for the encouragement of literary achievement, the upholding of professional standards, and social contact with other writers. Programme of speakers includes well-known people from the world of publishing, editing and broadcasting, as well as publicists, agents and authors in a variety of fields. Publishes a magazine for members three times a year.
V P

Society to Support Home Confinements
Lydgate, 67 Lydgate Lane, Wolsingham, Bishop Auckland, Co Durham DL13 3HA
0388-528044
Contact Margaret Whyte
Supports, advises and assists women who want a home confinement but who meet with difficulties in arranging midwifery attendance. Provides an advice and information service; organises local support groups and local agents.
B V

Solicitors Family Law Association (SFLA)
PO Box 302, Keston, Kent BR2 6EZ
0689-50227
Contact Mary l'Anson
Aims to promote a constructive rather than an aggressive or angry approach to resolving the problems flowing from marriage breakdown. Provides continuing education and

training for solicitors working in the field of family law. Responds to and initiates proposals for reform and development of the law, court structure, and methods of resolving problems flowing from the breakdown of the marriage and co-habiting relationship. Supplies a list of solicitors in a particular area who are members of the association and have adopted a common code of practice.
B M(2,000) S(1) P

Soroptimist International of Great Britain and Ireland
127 Wellington Road South, Stockport, Cheshire SK1 3TS
061-480 7686   Fax 061-477 6152
Contact Kay Hindley
International organisation of service clubs for women who hold key positions in industry, the professions and other spheres. Provides opportunities for a wide exchange of ideas and experience. Clubs work on projects in the local community and adopt projects for study and action within the international programme.
***** B V M(16,000) S(5) P**

South Glamorgan Women's Workshop
Edena House, East Canal Wharf, Cardiff CF1 5AQ
0222-493351   Fax 0222-482122
Provides education and training for women who, due to their social or economic circumstances, are unable to gain employment for jobs in which women are under-represented or in new occupations; establishes centres where women may be trained in such employment.

South-West Women's Arts Network (SWWAN)
The Salem Chapel, Broadhempston, Totnes, Devon TQ9 6BD
0803-813293
Contact Josie Sutcliffe
Aims to make women's art more visible. Provides women artists of every discipline (and women interested in the arts) with support, criticism, information and advice. Promotes events, workshops, seminars, and encourages the continued development of women artists.
 V M(145) P

Spare Tyre
41a Camden Road, London NW1 9LR
071-482 2888
Contact Clair Chapman
A theatre company which aims to provide entertaining, humourous plays and cabarets to a primarily, but not exclusively, female audience. Performs in various settings, runs drama workshops, helps to set up young theatre companies.
M(4) S(4) P

SPLASH (Single Parent Links and Special Holidays)
19 North Street, Plymouth, Devon PL4 9AH
0752-674067
Contact Susan Thyer
Provides one-parent families with low-cost holidays in the UK and abroad, where they meet others in a similar situation. Arranges a wide

range of holidays, at any time of the year, including holidays for unaccompanied children in the school holidays. Organises subsidised holidays for special cases.
C V M(30) S(6) T(Gingerbread Holidays Trading Ltd) P

SPOD (Association to Aid the Sexual and Personal Relationships of People with a Disability)
286 Camden Road, London N7 0BJ
071-607 8851
Contact Morgan Williams
Provides an advisory and counselling service for disabled people in sexual difficulty; an information service for professional and voluntary workers among the disabled; education and training on the sexual aspects of disability. Produces leaflets, resource lists, information sheets and books.
C B S(3) P

Standing Conference of Women's Organisations (SCWO)
Cap d'Or, Widbourne Avenue, Torquay, Devon TQ1 2PQ
0803-296564
Contact Irene Jarmain
Works for the benefit of the community; promotes ideas or suggestions to assist women in particular.
* C B V M(200+) S(1) P

Stepfamily (National Stepfamily Association)
72 Willesden Lane, London NW6 7TA
071-372 0844(office) 071-372 0846 (counselling)
Contact Steve Balkam
National organisation which provides support, advice and information to all members of stepfamilies and those who work with them. Runs a telephone counselling service and local self-help groups. Encourages a positive image of stepfamilies and offers support for continued growth in family life. Publications and newsletters are available.
C B V M(1,000) S(2) P

Steroid Aid Group
PO Box 220, London E17 3JR
A self-help group for people suffering from the side effects of cortico steroids.
B V M(1,000) P

Stillbirth and Neonatal Death Society (SANDS)
28 Portland Place, London W1N 4DE
071-436 5881
Contact Roma Iskander
Offers support through self-help groups and befriending to parents bereaved by stillbirth or neonatal death. Also aims to encourage an increased awareness of the feelings and needs of bereaved parents within the health professions and the general pub lic.
* C B V M(200) S(6) P

Stonewall Housing Association
Unit W58, TEC, 560-568 High Road, London N17 9TA
081-885 2305
Runs hostels for young lesbians and gay men who have been made homeless due to the hostile reaction of others to their sexuality. Age range is 17-25. All accommodation is temporary; average stay in hostels is 12-18 months. At any time, over 50 per cent of residents are women, and 50 per cent are black or minority ethnic.
C

Stonewall Lobby Group Ltd (Stonewall)
2 Greycoat Place, London SW1P 1SB
071-222 9007 Fax 071-222 1412
Contact Tim Barnett
Aims to achieve fully equal legal rights for lesbians and gay men in the UK by providing information and support for legislators. Involved in UK and European parliamentary lobbying; and works with lesbian and gay men in all political parties.
* V(Y) M(20) S(2) P

Streetwise Youth Project
3b Langham Mansions, Earls Court Square, London SW5 9UP
071-373 4803 071-373 8860 (helpline)
Contact Tony Whitehead
Offers support, counselling and assistance to young people for whom prostitution is a problem. Liaises with, and represents young people to the police, the probation service, the courts and parents.
C V S(1) P

Student Christian Movement Women's Network
186 St Paul's Road, Balsall Heath, Birmingham B12 8LZ
021-440 3000
Contact Liz Roe
Brings together young women from all denominations who meet to explore issues surrounding Christianity and feminism. Holds two or three weekend conferences per year.
C B P

Suzy Lamplugh Trust
14 East Sheen Avenue, London SW14 8AS
081-392 1839
Contact Elaine Bishop
Concerned with personal safety, the trust provides literature, videos and training packs on coping with aggression. Runs a helpline for friends and relatives of people who have gone missing. Markets an ozone-friendly personal alarm. Runs company training courses to alleviate aggression and stress in difficult circumstances.
C V S(4) P

Time Off for Women (TO)
King's Cross Women's Centre, 71 Tonbridge Street, London WC1H 9DZ
071-837 7509
Contact Anne Neale
International grassroots women's actions held annually to press governments to implement the 1985 UN decision to count all women's waged and unwaged work in every country's GNP. Jointly co-ordinated by the organisations in the International Wages for Housework

campaign. Produces anti-racist, anti-sexist children's exhibition and teachers' resource pack.
C B V(Y) P

Townswomen's Guilds
Chamber of Commerce House, 75 Harborne Road, Birmingham B15 3DA
021-456 3435 Fax 021-452 1890
Contact Rosie Styles
Aims to advance the education of women, irrespective of race, creed and party, so as to enable them to make their best contribution to the common good; and to provide a common meeting ground for social and recreational pursuits, with a view to improving the conditions of life for women. There are 2,300 Guilds grouped in 114 Federations in England, Scotland, Wales and Northern Ireland. National projects include consumer work, environmental studies, energy conservation, problems of inner cities, teaching communication skills. Activities with Guilds cover social studies, music, drama, arts and crafts, current affairs and sports.
C B M(120,000) S(16) P

Toxoplasmosis Trust
Garden Studios, 11-15 Betterton Street, London WC2H 9BP
071-379 0344 Fax 071-379 0801
Contact Philippa Wyn-Evans
Aims to promote the screening of women for toxoplasmosis, in particular during pregnancy. Also provides advice and counselling for women with a current infection during pregnancy and those with infected children.
C V M(14) P

Trades Union Congress
Congress House, Great Russell Street, London WC1B 3LS
071-636 4030 Fax 071-636 0632
Contact K Carberry
Seventy-eight British trade unions affiliate to the TUC, which co-ordinates policy and campaigns. Equal rights department spearheads the work of the TUC on women and black people concentrating mainly on employment questions such as equal pay, harassment, childcare, discrimination law and involvement of women and black people in unions.
B P

Transvestite/Transsexual Support Group (TV/TS Group)
2 French Place, off Bateman's Row, London E1 6JB
071-729 1466
Contact Adele Johns
Aims to advance public education and advice to transvestities and transsexuals, and all who have contact with them, via its helpline, correspondence, and face-to-face discussion. There are also weekend supportive meetings. The Group has close links with members of the medical profession specialising in the field.
* C B V M(1,000+) S(1) P

Trust for the Study of Adolescence
23 New Road, Brighton, East Sussex BN1 1WZ
0273-680281
Contact Dr John Coleman
Research and publications organisation which seeks to empower parents, especially mothers, in their relationships with their teenage children. Offers advice

and information through the 'Tapes for Parents' series, and is undertaking research work with teenage mothers.
C V P

Twins and Multiple Births Association (TAMBA)
51 Thicknall Drive, Pedmore, Stourbridge, West Midlands
DY9 0YH
0384-373642
Contact Mary Lowe
Offers individual and local-group support to families with twins, triplets or multiple-birth children; also promotes public and professional awareness of their needs. Produces literature; holds study days and conferences. Includes Supertwins Group, T wins with Special Needs Group and Bereavement Support Group.
* C B V P

Union of Catholic Mothers of England and Wales
12 Washington Avenue, St Leonards-on-Sea, East Sussex
TN37 7TG
0424-853384
Contact Terri Coombs
Aims to help Catholic married women to appreciate the sacramental character, responsibility and permanence of marriage, and to live in unselfish love observing the laws of God and His Church. Assists them to bring up their children as practising Catholics and public-spirited citizens. Teaches and defends Christian values in family life and ensures for their children a Catholic education.
C B V P

Union of Turkish Women in Britain (UTWB)
110 Clarence Road, London E5 8JA
081-985 4072
Contact Omur Aydin
Provides an advice, translation and interpretation service for Turkish-speaking women in Britain. A campaign against deportations has been organised. Runs educational seminars, cultural and sporting activities with the help of volunteers.
V M(200) S(7) P

United Kingdom Federation of Business and Professional Women (BPW)
23 Ansdell Street, London W8 5BN
071-938 1729
Contact Jean Skinner
Aims to promote a free and responsible society in which all women take an active part in decision-making at all levels; to determine, work for and maintain fair opportunities in education and training; to encourage co-operation and foster understanding among women throughout the world.
* B M(10,000) S(4) P

United Kingdom Home Economics Federation
8 Alms Hill Crescent, Sheffield
S11 9QZ
0742-362654
Contact P M Marshall
Aims to promote the development of home economics; to consider matters of common interest to its constituent bodies; to provide an organisation which can speak for home economics nationally and internationally.
* C V P

VDU Workers' Rights Campaign
City Centre, 32-35 Featherstone Street, London EC1Y 8QX
071-608 1338
Contact Irene Hamilton
Aims to seek legislative change and increase public awareness of the need to protect the health of VDU workers by limiting the time spent on VDUs and ensuring the right of prospective parents to transfer away from VDU work. Campaigns and lobbies among MPs, researchers and medical specialists, trades unions, women's groups and community groups. Organises conferences, dayschools, workshops; publishes information sheets and other materials.
V L P

Victims' Help Line
St Leonard's, Nuttall Street, London N1 5LZ
071-729 1226 (office)
071-729 1252 (24-hour helpline)
Contact Michael Damase
Runs 24-hour helpline to assist, nationwide and locally, any victim of any crime, especially women and other members of society who do not report crimes even against themselves to the police.
C V M(20) S(3)

Vineyard Project
Congregational Church, The Vineyard, Richmond, Surrey TW10 6AQ
081-940 2965
Community-based drop-in centre for the healing of loneliness. Relaxation classes to help combat stress and tranquiliser-withdrawal support group. Tues, 2.15 pm and Wed, 8.15pm.
V

Wages Due Lesbians (WDL)
King's Cross Women's Centre, 71 Tonbridge Street, London WC1H 9DZ
071-837 7509
Contact Anne Neale
Organisation of black and white lesbian women in the Wages for Housework campaign. Defends the rights of lesbian mothers to custody of their children; campaigns against all forms of legal, social and financial discrimination against lesbian women, and for economic independence of all women. Promotes awareness of lesbian women's contribution to the black/women's/peace/welfare/anti-rape movements.
B V(Y) P

Wages for Housework Campaign (WFHC)
King's Cross Women's Centre, 71 Tonbridge Street, London WC1H 9DZ
071-837 7509
Contact Selma James
Network of Third World and metropolitan women that campaigns to gain recognition and compensation for all the unwaged work done by women; to be paid by governments through dismantling the military-industrial complex. Circulates international petition available in 22 languages and braille; co-ordinates annual 'Time Off for Women' actions.
B V(Y) P

War Widows' Association of Great Britain
81 Gargrave Road,
Skipton-in-Craven, North Yorks
BD23 1QN
0756-793719
Contact Peggy Rigby
Works on behalf of all war widows, informing members on matters concerning their welfare.
M(4,000) P

We Welcome Small Children National Campaign
93a Belsize Lane, London NW3 5AY
071-586 3453 Fax 071-586 4662
Contact Julie Jaspert
Co-ordinates individuals and groups nationwide who are campaigning locally for improved facilities in public places, shops, restaurants, etc and more welcoming attitudes to carers with small children.
B V M(200) P

West Indian Women's Association
391-393 Chapter Road, London NW2 5NG
081-459 4961
Contact Garth Williams
Runs a women's group, offers help and advice on matters such as housing and welfare rights; organises an after-school junior club for 8- to 15-year-old age group, and a pensioners' club. Runs a badminton club, dance group and various cultural activities, summer playschemes, Employment Training programmes and nursery provision.
C B M(212) S(14) P

WinVisible: Women with Visible and Invisible Disabilities
King's Cross Women's Centre,
71 Tonbridge Street, London
WC1H 9DZ
071-837 7509
Contact Claire Glasman
UK-wide network of women of different races, lesbian and non-lesbian, with visible and invisible disabilities. Campaigns for economic independence, mobility, access and housing; for the right to have children and for abortion rights; against welfare cuts, racism, rape, nuclear and other military-industrial pollution.
V(Y) P

Womankind (Worldwide)
122 Whitechapel High Street, London
E1 7PT
071-247 6931 Fax 071-247 9432
Contact Lee Foley
Promotes awareness of the issues of women in developing countries through educational materials and workshops, fundraising and supporting women's groups.
* C B V S(5) P

Women Against Fundamentalism
BM Box 2706, London WC1 3XX
081-571 9595
A network which challenges the rise of fundamentalism in all religions; defends women against attacks by fundamentalists; provides refuges and protection for women experiencing violence inside and outside the home; disseminates information about fundamentalist activities affecting women and attempts to organise against them.
V P

Women Against Rape (WAR)
King's Cross Women's Centre,
71 Tonbridge Street, London
WC1H 9DZ
071-837 7509
Contact Lisa Longstaff
Support and advice to women surviving rape and other violence. Campaigns to end rape in all its forms including rape in marriage, racist sexual assault of black women and sexual abuse of power and authority. Presses for increased resources for rape survivors and for rape prevention through improvements in welfare, housing and other provision; for better treatment of rape survivors by the police and courts; and for changes in the law.
V(Y) S(1) P

Women Against Sexual Harassment (WASH)
242 Pentonville Road, London
N1 9UN
071-833 0222
Contact Louise Noakes
Provides support and advice for women who have been sexually harassed, particularly at work. Advises a wide range of groups on policy and codes of practice in the workplace. Campaigns for sexual harassment to be recognised as a serious health hazard, and for changes in the law.
C V M(100) S(1)

Women and Manual Trades (WAMT)
52-54 Featherstone Street, London
EC1Y 8RT
071-251 9192
Contact Mavis Williams
Gives advice and information to women training and working in the trades and to careers officers; publishes a listing of self-employed tradeswomen available to do work in homes and offices. Produces quarterly newsjournal with interviews, news, conference reports, job and course listing; manual on where to go for trades training; posters, video, exhibition, general information on women and the skilled trades.
B V S(5) P

Women and the Media
c/o Allanbank House, Greenloaning, Dunblane, Perthshire
0786-88200
Contact Isabel Bryce
Promotes greater participation by women in the media and improved coverage of women by the press. The organisation aims to make its own news and encourage editors to re-examine the question 'What is news?'.
V

Women and Training
120 London Road, Gloucester
GL1 3PL
0452-309330
Contact Christine Thompson
Aims to consider areas of need and to stimulate innovation in training for women by organising conferences and workshops; disseminating information and experience of successful strategies, techniques and

methods; producing a quarterly newsletter and establishing regional groups and activities.
V M(14,000) S(4) P

Women Architects Group of the RIBA
RIBA, 66 Portland Place, London W1N 4AD
071-580 5533   Fax 071-255 1541
Contact Sheila Miller
Promotes the specific interests of women in the profession. The group reports to the membership committee of the RIBA.
C B

Women Artists' Slide Library
Economic History Department, Liverpool University, 8 Abercromby Square, Liverpool L69 3BX
051-794 2416
Contact Dr Pat Hudson
Supports, documents and promotes the work of women artists, past and present. The slide collection contains over 20,000 slides divided into contemporary, historical and documentary sections; library open Tuesday-Friday 10 am-5 pm. Produces bi-monthly publication, diary containing the work of 43 contemporary women artists, plus postcards, greetings cards and wrapping paper.
C V P

Women for Improved Transport (WIT)
12 Bartholomew Road, London NW5 2LL
071-267 8136
Contact Hilary Torrance
Collects the views of women who use London Transport and conducts surveys into its operation with particular regard to the needs of women on matters of safety and access. Maintains contact with London Regional Transport and other transport campaigning groups; holds meetings, answers enquiries, provides speakers, briefs the media; offers support to women who wish to campaign on local issues.
M(40)

Women Heritage and Museums (WHAM)
Weybridge Museum, Church Street, Weybridge, Surrey KT13 8DE
0932-843573
Contact April Whincop
Promotes positive images of women in museums; provides a forum for debate on women's heritage; campaigns for equal opportunities in museums; combats discrimination on grounds of race, age, disability or sexual oritentation. Holds conferences and publishes a newsletter.
B V M(320) P

Women in Economic and Social History
PO Box 147, University of Liverpool, Liverpool L69 3BX
051-794 2413
Contact Dr Pat Hudson
Holds annual workshop in London; is compiling a directory to include all women who practise any kind of economic or social history and men who study women's history. New volunteers and participants are always welcome.
V P

Women in Education: The National Association
PO Box 149, Preston, Lancs
PR2 1HF
Contact Secretary
Seeks to promote equal opportunities, rights and responsibilities in the world of education and to remove discrimination based on sex, whether in law, practice or custom.
B V P

Women in Enterprise (WE)
St Gabriels House, 24 Laburnam Road, Wakefield, West Yorks
WF1 3QS
0924-361789 Fax 0924-382707
Contact Kay Smith
Offers support to self-employed women and to women setting up or running a business. Provides information on finance and sources of advice; publicises achievements; develops and promotes training; carries out research.
B V M(1,200) S(3) P

Women in Management
64 Marryat Road, Wimbledon, London SW19 5BN
081-944 6332
Contact Elizabeth Harman
Promotes the art and science of management; provides and encourages education in the principles of management. Runs annual evening programme of training and development, plus workshops; networks for small businesses and career changers.
* C B V M(800) S(1) P

Women in Publishing (WIP)
c/o 12 Dyott Street, London
WC1A 1DF
071-485 5002
Contact Information Officer
Provides a forum for the discussion of ideas, trends and subjects of interest to women in the publishing trades; encourages networking and mutual support among women; supports and publicises women's achievements and successes; promotes the status of women within publishing; offers training courses, monthly meetings, annual conferences and monthly newsletter.
B V M(500+) P

Women in Theology (WIT)
110 Glengall Road, London
NW6 7HH
071-372 3322
Contact Diane Brewster
Provides opportunities for doing theology from a feminist perspective; explores both experienced-based and academic styles of learning; fosters the use of inclusive language; and encourages new ways of worship.
C B V M(300) P

Women in Training
12 Denmark Grove, Alexandra Park, Nottingham NG3 4JG
0602-606615
Contact Lesley Cramman
Training consultancy which specialises in working with women who are considering a return to the workplace. Also runs courses for women already in employment, e.g. professional and personal development, assertiveness training, confidence-building, developing a

women's managerial style, etc.; all courses are tailored to the needs of course members.

Women into Business
Suite 46, Westminster Palace Gardens, Artillery Row, London SW1P 1RR
071-976 7262 Fax 071-976 7016
Contact Angela Browning
Aims to give women a higher national profile by acknowledging and publicising their business achievements in publications. Also organises teach-ins, seminars and conferences for existing and potential businesswomen. Lobbies government for more favourable conditions for businesswomen.
P

Women Returners' Network
Garden Cottage, Youngsbury, Ware, Herts SG13 0TZ
0920-464337
Contact Margaret Johnson
Aims to facilitate women's re-entry into education, training and employment through promoting opportunities, providing information, producing publications, encouraging local network formation, encouraging providers of education to meet women returners' needs, encouraging employers to undertake schemes to facilitate retention and re-entry.
C B V M(450) S(2) P

Women Welcome Women (WWW)
Granta, 8a Chestnut Avenue, High Wycombe, Bucks HP11 1DJ
0494-439481
Contact Frances Alexander
Fosters international friendship by enabling women of different countries to visit one another. Aims to learn how other women live; to extend the vision of women and their families; to become part of the international community of one world.
V M(650) P

Women Working Worldwide
2-4 Oxford Road, Manchester M1 5QA
Contact Angela Hale
Supports the struggle of women workers through international networking, information exchange and public information. Fundraises to support specific projects concerned with the textile and garment industry and the electronics industry.
B V M(12) P

Women's Aid Federation (England)
PO Box 391, Bristol BS99 7WS
0272-420611 (admin) 0272-428368 (helpline:10 am-10 pm weekdays)
Provides advice, information and temporary refuge for women and their children, on request, who are threatened by mental, emotional, or physical violence, harassment, or sexual abuse. 120 autonomous, locally-based member groups provide information, advice and refuge. National office provides helpline service and information and publications to the general public, and resources to member groups.
* C B V P

Women's Alcohol Centre (part of Alcohol Recovery Project)
66a Drayton Park, London N5 1ND
071-226 4581
Contact Marcia Cummings
Offers a comprehensive service to women who are having difficulties caused by alcohol. Offers individual counselling, practical information about alcohol and its effects on health, group meetings to discuss problem drinking; runs a meeting place; mai ntains a residential service; organises workshops; provides a creche facility.
C V S(4) P

Women's Centre
19a North Street Arcade, Belfast BT1 1PA
0232-243363
Contact Clare McLaughlin
Offers information, advice and support for women and women's groups. Lobbies for women's issues and better provision for women. Provides mobile creche and community outreach; organises classes on community care and speakers on other subjects, as requested.
C B V P

Women's Corona Society
Commonwealth House,
18 Northumberland Avenue, London WC2N 5BJ
081-839 7908
Contact Ellen Svoboda
Provides information, advice and personal contacts for families and single peolpe going to live in a country other than their own and welcomes overseas visitors and students to Britain. Publishes information booklets; organises courses; provides an escort service for members' children; maintains a panel of women speakers; holds conferences in London, and social functions for members and friends.
C M(7,000) P

Women's Development Agency (ADVO WDA)
20 Haymill Close, Stockdove Way, Perivale, Greenford, Middx UB6 7TJ
Contact Matilda Nantogmah
Holds meetings, seminars and conferences on women and development; fundraises; disseminates information. Runs national project on economic development - job creation and educational training in job-related skills.
B V T(Women-ADV Trading Co.)

Womens Employment Enterprise and Training Unit (WEETU)
The Glass House, 9-13 Wensum Street, Norwich NR3 1LA
0603-615200 Fax 0603-613500
Contact Kay Sanderson
Offers a free drop-in advice service to the women of Norwich, operating two days a week at the local advice centre. Also gives telephone advice and acts as a lobbying organisation on women's employment and training issues. Produces quarterly newsletter.
V P

Women's Engineering Society (WES)
Imperial College of Science and Technology, Dept of Civil Engineering, Imperial College Road, London SW7 2BU
071-589 5111 ext 4731

Contact G Maxwell
Promotes the study and practice of engineering among women, and supports and encourages them when they have entered the profession. Offers members the opportunity to meet other women engineers locally, nationally and internationally. Activities include annual conference, local meetings, careers information, student group meetings, lectures and quarterly journal.
B M(700) S(1) P

Women's Enterprise Development Agency (WEDA)
Aston Science Park, Love Lane, Aston Triangle, Birmingham B7 4BJ
021-359 0981 Fax 021-359 0433
Contact Pat Aduwa-French
Helps to release the energies of enterprising women and supports new ways of generating women's self-employment through a network of local agencies around the UK. Provides single-sex business training in management and financial control; techniques for successful expansion and for raising capital investment; plus the basics for start-up businesses. Also carries out research and runs workshops.
B V(Y) M(15) S(3) P

Women's Farm and Garden Association
175 Gloucester Street, Cirencester, Glos GL7 2DP
0285-658339
Contact M G Conu
Unites women involved or interested in agriculture, horticulture and allied subjects. Promotes the study and practice of these professions, and offers help and advice. Represents the views and interests of women at national and international level. Holds regional meetings, plus residential conferences and meetings; runs an employment service; produces regular newsletters and other publications.
C B M(300) S(2) P

Women's Farming Union
Crundalls, Matfield, Tonbridge, Kent TN12 7EA
0892-722803
Contact Joan Cremer
Speaks directly to consumers on the contribution farmers and farming make to the country's economy and of the benefit to be obtained from the variety of choice and the freshness of home-produced food.
* B V(Y) M(2,000) P

Women's Gas Federation
17 Grosvenor Crescent, London SW1X 7ES
071-235 2056
Contact Diana Beauchamp
Acts as a two-way link between the gas industry and the community. Non-commercial; branch programmes are related to the home in its widest aspect. Works with other organisations at branch, regional and national level.
* B V P

Women's Health and Reproductive Rights Information Centre
52-54 Featherstone Street, London EC1Y 8RT
071-251 6580 Fax 071-608 0928
Provides information and support to help women make informed decisions about their own health. The

centre offers a telephone and postal enquiry service, an extensive reference library, and a wide range of leafets and quarterly newsletter on women's health.
* C V P

Women's Health Concern (WHC)
PO Box 1629, London W8 6AU
071-938 3932 Fax 071-376 0879
Contact Jean Jenkins
Seeks to redress the ignorance and neglect of gynaecological and hormonal problems of women. Source of information and advice about the menopause, hormone replacement therapy (HRT), osteoporosis, answering more than 70,000 enquiries a year. Organises medical symposia and courses for nurses; provides professional counselling and publications.
C B V M(10,000) S(14) P

Women's Health Information and Support Centre (WHISC)
Junction 7, Hazelwood Road,
Northampton NN1 1LG
0604-39723
Contact Pat Quedley
Disseminates health information to women in order to enable them to take better care of themselves and their families. Educates, counsels and supports women, both as clients and professionals, on a wide range of issues affecting women's health. Runs a national information and advice service. Carries out research. Provides impartial and confidential counselling, pregnancy testing and health information in a relaxed, informal setting.
V S(1) P

Women's Health Network
National Community Health Resource, 57 Chalton Street, London NW1 1HU 071-383 3841
Contact Justine Pepperrel
Based within the community health movement, the network is open to anyone who wants to empower women to take control of their own health and healthcare. Aims to link groups and individuals and provide support for their work; offers advice, information, training and a newsletter.
C B V P

Women's History Conference Centre
Middlesex Polytechnic, Queensway, Enfield, Middx EN3 4SF
081-368 1299
Contact Gillian Darcy
The Centre organises conferences on a variety of subjects on women and the past; also maintains a database of those people working on research in women's history. List of researchers and their interests is available.
V P

Women's Holiday Centre
The Old Vicarage,
Horton-in-Ribblesdale, near Settle,
North Yorks BD23 0HD
0729-6207
Offers cheap holidays for women and children (boys up to 10) in the Yorkshire dales; private and communal rooms, open fires; food included in cost of stay (cook your own); wheelchair accessible downstairs; large garden. All women welcome, both individuals and groups.
C V

Women's Inter-Church Consultative Committee (WICC)
2 Pentargon Road, Boscastle, North Cornwall PL35 0EW
08405-444
Contact Thelma Stewart
Represents every denomination of the church, women's organisations, student Christian movement and the YWCA. Aims to raise the status and participation of women within the church, working towards the equal partnership of women and men. Holds day conferences open to everyone throughout Great Britain; publishes workpacks and leaflets.
C V M(35) P

Women's International League for Peace and Freedom (British Section) (WILPF)
157 Lyndhurst Road, Worthing, Sussex BN11 2DG
Contact Margot Miller
Brings together women of different political and philosophical inclinations to study, publicise and help abolish the political, social, economic and psychological causes of war. Part of an international network with sections in 25 countries.
B V M(450) S(1) P

Women's League of Health and Beauty (Health and Beauty Exercise)
Walter House, 418-422 The Strand, London WC2R 0PP
071-240 8456
Contact Peter Hutton
Aims to advance physical education for women based upon the system of remedial and recreative exercises initiated by Mrs Bagot Stack in 1930, consisting of training in correct body alignment; appreciation of the art of movement; training in relaxation and breathing techniques; group exercise to music. Part-time training courses are available for girls who wish to take up League teaching.
C B V M(19,000) S(20) P

Women's Legal Defence Fund
29 Great James Street, London WC1N 3ES
071-831 6890 Fax 071-405 7239
Provides advice and information, case preparation and negotiation, representation and a 'best friend', for sex discrimination and equal pay cases. The service is free at the point of delivery.
C B V P

Women's Media Resource Project (WMRP)
85 Kingsland High Street, London E8 2PB
071-254 6536
Contact Mary Fahey
Provides a comprehensive service for women involved in the audio visual media with a view to expanding their participation in both the commercial and community sectors. The project consists of a 16-track recording studio and a 30-seat screening space for videos, films and discussions for women; both the resource and the equipment are available for hire.
C V M(40) S(6) P

Women's National Cancer Control Campaign
1 South Audley Street, London
W1Y 5DQ
071-499 7532
Contact Campaign Secretary
Promotes screening and early detection of cancer. Runs mobile clinics for cervical screening and encourages breast screening. Provides speakers, literature and telephone helpline service.
* C B V M(200) S(6) P

Women's National Commission
Government Offices, Horse Guards Road, London SW1P 3AL
071-270 5903 Fax 071-270 5828
Aims to ensure by all possible means that the informed opinions of women are given their due weight in the deliberations of government.
V P

Women's Natural Health Centre
1 Hillside, Highgate Road, London NW5 1QT
071-482 3293 (for appointments, 9.30 am-1 pm)
Provides complementary therapies to women on a low income and their children. A group of professionally trained women practitioners offers acupuncture, herbalism, healing, counselling, homeopathy, massage, osteopathy, reflexology and psychotherapy.
M(5)

Women's Nutritional Advisory Service
PO Box 268, Hove, East Sussex
BN3 1RW
0273-771366 Fax 0273-820576
Contact Michelle Apsey
Provides a postal advisory service for PMT sufferers, women with menopausal problems or problems relating to the contraceptive pill. Runs a nutritional programme to handle these problems. Also has two PMT clinics.
V

Women's Resource Centre (WCR) (formerly Women's Education Group)
Holborn Centre, 1-3 Princeton Street, London WC1R 4BH
071-242 6807
Contact Gloria Walsh
Encourages and supports anti-sexist and anti-racist initiatives by and for women by offering meeting space, facilities for the publication of newsletters and resources promoting positive images of women worldwide. Runs workshops and courses, gives advice, information and support to individual women and groups, and provides a video camera and use of office equipment.
V S(4) P

Women's Royal Voluntary Service (WRVS)
234-244 Stockwell Road, London SW9 9SP
071-416 0146 Fax 071-416 0148
Contact Information Services Co-ordinator
Assists government departments and other statutory bodies in organising and carrying out welfare and

emergency work for the community. Provides meals-on-wheels services for young families, elderly and disabled people; and non-medical services in hospitals. Runs feeding, clothing and rest centres in national and local emergencies.
* B V P

Women's Sports Foundation (WSF)
c/o London Women's Centre, Wesley House, 4 Wild Court, London WC2B 5AU
071-831 7863
Contact Ruth Jordan
Builds up a national grass-roots network of women interested in sport; works to encourage women of all backgrounds and abilities to participate in sport and to ensure that the opportunities for them to do so are made available; campaigns.
* B V(Y) S(2) P

Women's Tapeover
c/o 66 Oakfield Road, London N4 4LB
Contact R Ni Mhaille
Aims to make available to blind and partially-sighted women information that is currently only available in print. Produces a monthly taped magazine consisting of articles from the feminist press. Women's Tapeover is produced by and for blind and partially-sighted women. Sighted women volunteers are welcome to help edit, read and record the magazine.
V P

Women's Therapy Centre
6-9 Manor Gardens, London N7 6LA
071-263 6200 (1.30-4 pm, Mon-Fri, plus answerphone)
Contact Advice and Information
Offers a psychotherapy service to women. Aims to be accessible particularly to women in need of an all-women service, for example incest survivors, rape victims; also to working-class women, black women and women from ethnic minorities, women with disabilities, and lesbians. Offers training courses for professionals.
* C V M(12) S(12) P

Work Injured Nurses Group (WING)
Royal College of Nursing of the UK, 20 Cavendish Square, London W1M 0AB
071-409 3333 ext 308
Fax 071-408 0190
Contact Jill Salt
Advises work-injured nurses about their rights and facilities for rehabilitation. Raises funds for treatment of work-injured nurses. Runs two conferences a year. Provides a telephone-link scheme to reduce isolation.
C B V M(358) S(2) P

Working for Childcare/Workplace Nurseries
77 Holloway Road, London N7 8JZ
071-700 0281
Contact Delyth Morgan
Encourages the development of workplace nurseries to meet the needs of working parents and the social, educational and welfare requirements of their children. Promotes the development of all work-related childcare. Undertakes

research and provides information. Supplies information and advice on setting up workplace nurseries. Offers a consultancy service for employers and organisations in need of specific advice on establishing workplace childcare.
V M(300) S(7) P

Working Mothers' Association (WMA)
77 Holloway Road, London N7 8JZ
071-700 5771   Fax 071-700 1105
Contact Information Officer
Provides information and advice about childcare provision to enable working parents to make the best possible choice of care for their child. Provides information about the needs of working parents to other interested organisations and employers, and works for the improvement of childcare provision for children from birth to adolescence. Co-ordinates local groups and puts mothers in touch with them.
* C B V M(2,000) S(3) P

Young Women's Christian Association of Great Britain
Clarendon House, 52 Cornmarket Street, Oxford OX1 3EJ
0865-726110
Contact Elizabeth Sharples
A Christian, ecumenical and international organisation. Maintains links with YWCAs in other countries through the World YWCA in Geneva. Provides residential accomodation, primarily for young women, social and educational programmes in clubs and centres, detached youth and community work, young wives' work, residential courses for young women Facilities are available without distinction of race, nationality, politics or religion.
* C B V(Y) P

Appendix 1 Umbrella bodies

VOLUNTARY ORGANISATIONS — GENERAL

Information about national voluntary organisations in Great Britain (many of whom are concerned to work with women, or who have equal opportunities specialists on their staff) can be obtained from:

Information and Technology Team,
National Council for Voluntary Organisations
26 Bedford Square, London
WC1B 3HU
071-636 4066 Fax 071-436 3188

For information about community-based self-help organisations, contact:

National Federation of Self-Help Organisations,
150 Townmead Road, London
SW6 2RA
071-731 8440
See also page 36.
Information about local voluntary organisations, and about local schemes for volunteering, may be available from your local library, or from community workers, or from the social services department of your local town, district or county councils. The following organisations may also be able to help you:

Your local council for voluntary service
(address available from:
National Association of Councils for Voluntary Service

PO Box 717, Sheffield S1 1NL
0742-786636

Your local citizens advice bureau
(address in local phone book)

For information about voluntary organisations in Scotland, Wales and Northern Ireland, contact the following bodies:

Scottish Council for Voluntary Organisations
18-19 Claremont Crescent, Edinburgh
EH7 4QD
031-556 3882

Wales Council for Voluntary Action
Llys Ifor, Crescent Road, Caerffili,
Canol Morgannwg CF8 1XL
0222-869224

Northern Ireland Council for Voluntary Action
127 Ormeau Road, Belfast BT7 1SH
0232-321224

Women's alliances are developing in Scotland, Wales and Northern Ireland. These alliances have been co-operating with NAWO (see page 31) to form a federal relationship giving a unified voice to all women in the UK.
Women's alliances in Scotland, Wales and Northern Ireland can be contacted through:

Women's Forum Scotland
c/o Lesley Sutherland, 290 Bath Street, Glasgow G2 4LD
041-332 7321 (work) 041-334 9983 (home) Fax 041-332 6157

Wales Women's Euro Network
c/o Marlene Thomas, 26 Plantation Drive, Croes-y-Ceiliog, Cymbran, Gwent NP44 2AN
06333-838838 (work) 06333-5067 (home)

Northern Ireland Women's European Platform
c/o Bronagh Hinds, NICVA, 127 Ormeau Road, Belfast BT7 1SH
0232-230 220 (work)
Fax 0232-438 350

ORGANISATIONS SPECIFICALLY FOR WOMEN

Equal Opportunities Commission
Overseas House, Quay Street, Manchester M3 3HN
061-833 9244 Fax 061-835 1657

National Alliance of Women's Organisations
279-281 Whitechapel Road, London E1 1BY
071-247 7052
See also page 31.

National Council of Women of Great Britain
36 Danbury Street, London N1 8JU
071-354 2395
See also page 35.

Women's International Resource Centre
173 Archway Road, London N6 5BL
081-341 4403

Women's National Commission
Government Offices, Horse Guards Road, London SW1P 3AL
071-270 5903 Fax 071-270 5828
See also page 64.

Appendix 2 Women's centres

Birmingham Women's Centre
Devonshire House, High Street,
Digbeth, Birmingham B12 OLP
021-773 6952

Bristol Women's Centre
44 The Grove, Bristol BS1 4RB
0272-293575

Cambridge Women's Aid
PO Box 302, Cambridge
0223-460947

Cardiff Women's Centre
2 Coburn Street, Cathays, Cardiff
CF4 2BS
0222-383024

Derby Women's Centre
135 Green Lane, Derby DE1 1RZ
0332-41633

Edinburgh Women's Centre
61A Broughton Street, Edinburgh
EH1 3RY
031-557 3179

Exeter Women's Centre
94 Sidwell Street, Exeter EX4 6PH
0392-219982

Leeds Women's Centre
229 Woodhouse Lane, Leeds LS2 9LF
0532-421232

Leicester Women's and Homeless Centre
94 Belgrave Gate, Leicester LE1 3GR
0533-545559

Norwich Women's Centre
34 Exchange Street, Norwich
NR2 1AX
0603-628130

Nottingham Women's Centre
30 Chaucer Street, Nottingham
NG1 5LP
0602-411475

Oxford Women's Centre
35-37 Cowley Road, Oxford OX4 1HP
0865-245923

Plymouth Women's Centre
Virginia House, Peacock Lane,
Barbican, Plymouth PL4 0EQ
0752-261251

Reading Women's Information Centre
6 Silver Street, Reading RG1 2ST
0734-311939

WOMEN'S CENTRES IN GREATER LONDON

Asian Women's Action Group
18A Edison Road, London N8 8AE
081-341 2351/348 6900

Asian Women's Resource Centre
134 Minet Avenue, London
NW10 8AP
081-961 5701

Brent Women's Centre
232 Willesden High Road, London
NW10 2NX
081-459 7660

Deptford Women's Centre
74 Deptford High Street, London
SE8 4RT
081-692 9427

Enfield Women's Centre
31a Derby Road, Enfield, Middx
EN3 4AJ
081-443 1902

Hillingdon Women's Centre
333 Long Lane, Hillingdon, Middx
UB10 9JU
0895-59578

King's Cross Women's Centre
71 Tonbridge Street, London WC1H 9DZ
071-837 7509
See also page 23.

Kingston Women's Centre
169 Canbury Park Road, Kingston
KT2 6LG
081-541 1941/1964 (24-hour answerphone)

South Camden Women's Centre
90 Cromer Street, London WC1H 5DD
071-278 0120/837 8774

Southall Black Sisters
52 Norwood Road, Southall, Middx
UB2 4DW
081-571 9595

Southwark Women's Centre
Peckham High Street, London
SE15 4DY
071-701 2564/2468

Sutton Women's Centre
3 Palmerston Road, Sutton, Surrey
SN1 4QL
081-661 1991

Waltham Forest Women's Centre
109 Hoe Street, London E17 4SA
081-520 5318

Appendix 3 Crisis organisations

THE SAMARITANS

Provide a free, confidential, 24-hour telephone service for people in distress. The telephone number of your local branch will be at the front of your phone book, in the emergency numbers section. It will also be listed, under 'Samaritans', in the main A-Z entries. If you do not have a phone book (perhaps you are using a public callbox), ask the operator or Directory Enquiries to tell you the local Samaritans' number.

WOMEN'S REFUGES

There are women's refuges in many major towns and cities, which provide a temporary safe haven for women and children escaping from physical or mental violence, together with welfare advice and a range of counselling services. For obvious reasons, the addresses of these refuges are usually not publicised. For information about your nearest refuge, contact your local women's centre (see appendix 2) or:

Women's Aid Federation (England)
PO Box 391, Bristol BS99 7WS
0272-428368 (helpline); 0272-420611 (general enquiries)
See also page 59.

There is also:

Chiswick Family Rescue Ltd
PO Box 855, London W4 4JF
081-995 4430 (24-hour crisis line);
081-747 0133 (office)
An independent refuge, one of the pioneer bodies in this field.
See also page 11.

OTHER ORGANISATIONS

Crisis Counselling for Alleged Shoplifters (CCAS)
PO Box 1892, London NW4 4NX
081-202 5787; 071-722 3685;
081-958 8859 (after 7pm)
See also page 13.

London Lesbian Line (LLL)
BM Box 1514, London WC1N 3XX
071-251 6911
See also page 28.

London Rape Crisis Centre (LRCC)
PO Box 69, London WC1X 9NJ
071-837 1600 (counselling);
071-278 3965 (general enquiries)
See also page 28.

Parents Anonymous
Manor Gardens Centre, 6-9 Manor Gardens, London N7 6LA
071-263 8918 (24-hour)
See also page 41.

Victims' Help Line
St leonard's, Nuttall Street, London N1 5LZ
071-729 1252 (helpline);
071-729 1226 (general enquiries)

Appendix 4 Political organisations

Co-operative Women's Guild
342 Hoe Street, London E17 9PX
081-520 4902
See also page 12.

CONSERVATIVE PARTY

Women's Organiser, Conservative Central Office
32 Smith Square, London SW1P 3HF
071-222 9000

GREEN PARTY

Francis Hutchinson (organiser), Women's Network
Willow Bark, Riddlesden, Keighley, West Yorks BD30 5AN
0535-600356

LABOUR PARTY

Vicky Phillips, Women's Officer, Labour Party
150 Walworth Road, London SE17 1JT
071-703 0833

Shadow Ministry for Women
PO Box 1101, London SW1A 2HY

Social and Liberal Democrats

SLD Women's Organisation
Women's Office, 4 Cowley Street, London SW1P 3NB
071-222 3070

Appendix 5 International women's organisations

The organisations listed below represent the tip of the proverbial iceberg, but they should provide useful contact points for women in the UK seeking to learn from the experiences of women in other countries. Jane Grant's book *Sisters Across the Atlantic: A Guide to Networking in the US* (1988) (available from NAWO (see page 31)) gives a great deal of useful information about all these US organisations, and many others. Essential reading.

UNITED STATES

American Association of University Women
2401 Virginia Avenue NW
Washington DC 20037

Catalyst
250 Park Avenue S
New York, NY 10003

League of Women Voters of the US
1730 M Street NW
Washington DC 20036

National Federation of Business and Professional Women's Clubs Inc of the USA
2101 Massachusetts Avenue NW
Washington DC 20036

National Organisation for Women (NOW)
1401 New York Avenue NW
Washington DC 20005

National Women's Political Caucus
1275 K Street NW, Washington DC 20005

Women's Action Alliance Inc
370 Lexington Avenue, New York, NY 10017

Women's Way
125 South Ninth Street, Philadelphia, PA 19017

INTERNATIONAL

Branch for the Advancement of Women, UN Centre for Social Development and Humanitarian Affairs
Room 3 - 1283 Vienna International Centre, PO Box 500, A-1400
Vienna, Austria
'The main centre for the UN's work on women.' (Jane Grant)

European Forum of Socialist Feminists
Clare Crocker (UK contact), Garden Flat, 7 Acol Road, London NW6 3AA
071-328 5108

European Women's Lobby
Jacqueline de Groote, Co-ordinatrice, Avenue de Mercure 11, Btw 4-11809, Brussels 02217-9020

Women's alliances in Scotland, Wales and Northern Ireland (see appendix 1) have been co-operating with NAWO in connection with organising elections with UK representatives to the General Assembly of the European Women's Lobby.

International Alliance of Women
1st Floor, Jebb Wing, Regent's College, Regent's Park, London NW1 4NS
071-487 7437

International Women's Rights Action Watch
c/o Development Law and Policy Program, Centre for Population and Family Planning, Columbia University, 60 Haven Avenue, New York NY 10032, USA
Seeks to develop a world-wide of groups working for rights for women.

International Women's Tribune Centre
777 United Nations Plaza, New York NY 10017, USA
A non-governmental, not-for-profit international organisation for women, concerned particularly to help women and women's organisations in developing countries.

UN Commission on the Status of Women
Office of Secretariat Services for Economic and Social matters, One United Nations Plaza, New York, NY 10017, USA
The UN body officially responsible for women's issues.

Unifem – United Nations Development Fund for Women
Room 1120, 304 East 45th Street, New York, NY 10017, USA
Supports the involvement of women in development, and channelling funds to projects designed to benefit women.

Women Working Worldwide
Textile and Garment Project, Sociology Department, University of Manchester, Manchester M13 9PL
Supports the struggle of women workers worldwide for better pay and conditions.

Women's International League for Peace and Freedom (British Section)
157 Lyndhurst Road, Worthing, Sussex BN11 2DG

Appendix 6 Women in rural areas

Women living in rural areas very often have to face the problems of isolation. Many of the services that once provided a focal point for the community have disappeared. Shops, post offices, village schools, railway lines and bus routes have closed and many small churches share a vicar. It can be difficult to meet people to talk to, to share interests and enthusiasms with, or to turn to for help and support in times of difficulty.

Rural women also face problems of physical isolation – the nearest shopping centre, crèche, doctor's surgery, library or meeting place can be a long, awkward journey away. All too often, public transport is virtually non-existent. Without access to a car, rural women – particularly if they are elderly, unwell, or have young children – can become virtual prisoners in their own homes.

Other changes affecting rural women's lives include the centralisation of health and social services in the towns. Many cottage hospitals have closed and many rural GPs have amalgamated their practices. The balance of population is also changing. Many rural areas have experienced an influx of well-off professionals and retired people, and an outflow of unskilled younger people. The proportion of older people in rural areas is above the national average, and women are the majority of this group.

Employment patterns have changed as well. Many traditional jobs have disappeared, local wages are low and commuting is common. Many rural women are involved in the family farm business, often unpaid. While tourism in some areas has created new jobs, these are often seasonal and poorly paid. Rural women's wages are even lower than those of urban women. Even in the most apparently affluent areas, real poverty and deprivation exist, but they are mainly hidden. About one quarter of all rural households are living on or near the state defined poverty level, and the largest single category of rural poor is elderly women living alone.

To sum up, the main difficulties for rural women are:

- physical and social isolation
- lack of transport and distance
- lack of local services and choice
- employment difficulties
- lack of childcare
- access to information and advice

The organisations listed below can help rural women overcome some of the problems they face. Other forms of help may also be available. Many social services departments, local education authorities and rural community councils sponsor community groups or adult education classes in local centres. Ask at your nearest library, or phone the social services department (ask for community workers) of your district or county councils. In many villages, village hall committees arrange social functions, mother and baby groups, playgroups, and clubs for elderly people. Local churches are also active in these areas; look on your local church noticeboard or ask someone you know, or your local clergyman, what is going on. Local amenity societies, such as your county branch of the Council for the Preservation of Rural England, will arrange programmes of lectures, visits and social events. Your nearest library will give you the address of amenity societies active in your area. There will also be local branches of Friends of the Earth and Greenpeace. Phone their national headquarters (FOE: 071-490 1555, Greenpeace: 071-354 5100) for the name of local branch secretaries.

Transport to events can often be a problem; some local authorities sponsor unprofitable local bus services; others encourage community bus schemes or 'share a car' partnerships. Again, your local library should be able to help with information about what is on offer locally. Don't be afraid to make your transport needs known; many people are happy to offer lifts once they realise you need help

Last but not least, your local paper, and local shop windows, will be full of advertisements for 'coming events', often designed to raise money for a good cause. These events need as much public support as possible to make them a success. They can also be a good way of meeting other people, as well as offering the opportunity for an enjoyable outing.

Associated Country Women of the World
Vincent House, Vincent Square, London SW1P 2NB
071-834 8635 Fax 071-233 6205
See also page 3.

Farm Women's Club
Mrs Judy Steele (organiser), c/o *Farmers Weekly*, Greenfield House, 69-73 Manor Road, Wallington, Surrey SM6 ODE

081-661 4927
See also page 17.

National Alliance of Women's organisations
279-281 Whitechapel Road, London E1 7BT
071-247 7052
See also page 31.

Mothers' Union
Mary Sumner House, 24 Tufton Street, London SW1P 3RB
071-222 5533
See also page 31.

National Council of Women of Great Britain
36 Danbury Street, London N1 8JU
071-354 2395
See also page 35.

National Federation of Women's Institutes
104 New Kings Road, London SW6 4LY
071-371 9300 Fax 071-736 3652
See also page 36.

National Federation of Young Farmers Clubs
YFC Centre, National Agriculture Centre, Kenilworth, Warwicks, CV8 2LG
0203-696544

National Institute for Adult Continuing Education (NIACE)
47 New Walk, Leicester LE1 6TE
0533-551451

REPLAN
Adult Training Promotions Unit, Room 2/2, Department of Education and Science, Elizabeth House, 39 York Road, London SE1 7PH
071-934 0888

Women Returners' Network
Garden Cottage, Youngsbury, Ware, Herts, SG12 0TZ
0920-464337

Women's Environmental Network
287 City Road, London EC1V 1LA
071-490 2511

Women's Farm and Garden Association
175 Gloucester Street, Cirencester, Glos GL7 2DP
0285-658339
See also page 61.

Women's Farming Union
Crundalls, Matfield, Tonbridge, Kent TN12 7EA
0892-722803
See also page 61.

Women's Health Network
National Community Health Resource, 57 Charlton Street, London NW1 1HU
071-383 3841
See also page 62.

Women's Royal Voluntary Service (WRVS)
233-234 Stockwell Road, London SW9 9SP
071-733 3388 Fax 071-326 4240
See also page 65.

Workers Educational Association
9 Upper Berkeley Street, London W1H 8BY
071-402 5608

Young Women's Christian Association of Great Britain
Clarendon House, 52 Cornmarket Street, Oxford OX1 3EJ
0865-726110
See also page 66.

Appendix 7 Women and the family

Age Concern, England (National Council on Ageing)
1268 London Road, London
SW16 4EJ
081-679 8000 Fax 081-679 6069
Works to promote the welfare of all elderly people. Can refer enquirers to local groups.

Carers National Association
29 Chilworth Mews, London W2 3RG
071-724 7776
For anyone caring for a dependant relative or close friend.

Childcare Now
Wesley House, 4 Wild Court, London
WC2B 5AU
071-831 6632
A campaign set up to lobby for improved childcare facilities in the UK, in line with the recommendations of the European Commission's Childcare Network.

Exploring Parenthood
39-41 North Road, London N7 9DP
071-607 9647
See also page 16.

Gingerbread
35 Wellington Street, London
WC2E 7BN
071-240 0953
See also page 19.

Kids' Clubs Network (National Out of School Alliance)
279-281 Whitechapel Road, London
E1 1BY
071-247 3009 Fax 071-247 4490
See also page 24.

Maternity Alliance
15 Britannia Street, London
WC1X 9JP
071-837 1265
See also page 29.

National Childbirth Trust (NCT)
Alexandra House, Oldham Terrace,
London W3 6NH
081-992 8637 Fax 081-992 5929
See also page 33.

National Council for One Parent Families (NCOPF)
255 Kentish Town Road, London
NW5 2LX
071-267 1361 Fax 071-482 4851
See also page 34.

Relate – National Marriage Guidance
Herbert Gray College, Little Church Street, Rugby, Warwicks, CV21 3AP
0788-73421 Fax 0788-535007
See also page 45.

PARENTLINE – OPUS
Rayfa House, 57 Hart Road,
Thundersley, Essex SS7 3PD
0268-757077 Fax 0268-590590
Umbrella organisation of self-help groups for parents under stress. Can refer callers to local groups.

Working for Childcare/Workplace Nurseries*
77 Holloway Road, London N7 8JZ
071-700 0281
See also page 66.

Appendix 8 Women and health

Many organisations dealing with individual conditions and health-related topics that concern women are listed in the main directory. The following groups can offer general information and advice.

Association of Community Health Councils for England and Wales
30 Drayton Park, London N5 1PB
071-609 8405 Fax 071-700 1152

College of Health
St Margaret's House, 21 Old Ford Road, London E2 9PL
081-983 1225

Medical Women's Federation
Tavistock House North, Tavistock Square, London WC1H 9HX
071-387 7765
See also page 30.

Women's Health Concern (WHC)
PO Box 1629, London W8 6AU
071-938 3932 Fax 071-376 0879
See also page 62.

Women's Health and Reproductive Rights Information Centre
52-54 Featherstone Street, London EC1Y 8RT
071-251 6580 Fax 071-608 0928
See also page 62.

Women's Health Network
National Community Health Resource, 57 Charlton Street, London NW1 1HU
071-383 3841
See also page 62.

Women's National Cancer Control Campaign
1 South Audley Street, London W1Y 5DQ
071-499 7532
See also page 64.

Women's Natural Health Centre
1 Hillside, Highgate Road, London NW5 1QT
071-482 3293
See also page 64.

Women's Therapy Centre
6-9 Manor Gardens, London N7 6LA
071-263 6200
See also page 65.

Appendix 9 Women and history

Fawcett Library
City of London Polytechnic, Old Castle Street, London E1 7NT
071-247 5826
See also page 17.

Feminist Archive
Trinity Road Library, St Phillips, Bristol BS2 ONW
0272-350025
See also page 17.

Feminist Library and Information Centre
5 Westminster Bridge Road, London SE1 7XW
071-928 7789
See also page 18.

Pankhurst Trust
The Pankhurst Centre, 60-62 Nelson Street, Chorlton on Medlock, Manchester M13 9WP
061-273 5673
See also page 41.

Women Artists' Slide Library
Fulham Palace, Bishop's Avenue, London SW6 6EA
071-731 7618
See also page 57.

Women, Heritage and Museums (WHAM)
Weybridge Museum, Church Street, Weybridge, Surrey KT13 8DE
0932-843573
See also page 57.

Women in Economic and Social History
c/o Dr Pat Hudson, Department of Economic History, University of Liverpool, PO Box 147, Liverpool L69 3BX
051-794 2413
See also page 57.

Women's History Conference Centre
Middlesex Polytechnic, Queensway, Enfield, Middx EN3 4SF
081-368 1299
See also page 62.

Women's Studies Group 1500–1825
53 New Dover Road, Canterbury, Kent CT1 3DP
0227-462471

Appendix 10 Women and the media

RADIO AND TELEVISION
BBC (British Broadcasting Corporation)
Cherry Erlich, Equal Opportunities Officer
Broadcasting House, Portland Place, London W1A 1AA
071-580 4468
The BBC has stated that it is keen to encourage more women to progress to positions of responsibility within its organisation.
If you wish to comment on BBC TV or radio programmes for women, or about the portrayal of women in BBC programmes, write to the producer of the programme concerned, or to the Public Affairs Department of the BBC at the address above.

Independent radio and television
If you have a complaint about a broadcast programme there are official bodies to whom you can complain. The role of the Independent Broadcasting Authority (IBA) in regulating broadcasting has been taken over by the Broadcasting Standards Council as the new Independent Television Council (ITC) has a reduced regulatory role. The Broadcasting Standards Council will handle complaints from the public about the screen portrayal of violence, sex and standards of taste and decency. The Broadcasting Complaints Commission handles complaints of unjust or unfair treatment and allegations of unwarranted invasion of privacy in radio, television, cable and satellite. It is a statutory body and often adjudicates in cases where companies or professional bodies dispute the way they have been portrayed.

If you wish to find out how each independent radio or television company considers its programme planning in the light of women's interests and women's needs, or if you wish to comment on how women are portrayed on air or on screen, you should write to the individual television companies listed below, or to the umbrella body for local radio stations. About 50 new local radio stations have opened in recent years; there is great scope for women's interests to be considered in programme planning: not only do women, at home or at work, form a substantial part of the radio audience, but providing information about activities by and for local women could come to be seen as an important part of the radio companies' service to the local community.

National independent television

British Satellite Broadcasting
The Marcopolo Building, Chelsea Bridge, Queenstown Road, London SW8 4NQ
071-978 2222

Channel Four Television Co Ltd
60 Charlotte Street, London W1P 2AX
071-631 4444

Independent Television News
ITN House, 200 Gray's Inn Road,
London WC1X 8HB
071-833 3000

Sky Television
6 Centaurs, Business Park, Grant
Way, Isleworth, Middx TW7 5QD
071-782 3000

TV – am
Breakfast Television Centre, Hawley
Crescent, London NW1 8EF
071-267 4300

Regional independent television

Anglia Television
Anglia House, Norwich NR1 1JG
0603-615151

Border Television
The Television Centre, Carlisle
CA1 3NT
0228-25101

Central Independent Television
Central House, Broad Street,
Birmingham B1 2JP
021-643 9898

Channel Television
The Television Centre, St Helier,
Jersey, Channel Islands
0534-689999

Grampian Television
Queen's Cross, Aberdeen AB9 2XJ
0224-646464

Granada Television
Granada TV Centre, Manchester
M60 9EA
061-839 0454

HTV
The Television Centre, Culverhouse
Cross, Cardiff CF5 6XJ
0222-590590

London Weekend Television
South Bank Television Centre,
London SE1 9LT
071-620 1620

SC4
Welsh Fourth Channel Authority, Clos
Sophia, Caerdydd, CF1 9XY

Scottish Television
Cowcaddens, Glasgow G2 3PR
041-332 9999

Thames Television
Thames Television House, 306-316
Euston Road, London NW1 3BB
071-387 9494

TSW – Television South West
Derry's Cross, Plymouth, Devon
PL1 2SP
0752-663322

TVS Television
Television Centre, Southampton
SO9 5HZ
0703-634211

Tyne Tees Television
The Television Centre, City Road,
Newcastle upon Tyne, NE1 2AL
091-2610181

Ulster Television
Havelock House, Ormeau Road,
Belfast BT7 1EB
0232-328122

Yorkshire Television
The Television Centre, Leeds
LS3 1JS
0532-438283

Independent local radio umbrella body

Association of Independent Radio Contractors
Radio House, 46 Westbourne Grove,
London W2 5SH
071-727 2646

Children's television

British Action for Children's Television
21 Stephen Street, London W1P 1PL
Campaigns for a wide range of 'appropriate' children's programmes, in recognition of the positive role television can play in children's lives.

Formal complaints

The following organisation exists to investigate complaints about unfair or unjust treatment or about unwarranted infringement of privacy ONLY:

Broadcasting Complaints Commission
Grosvenor Gardens House, 35-37 Grosvenor Gardens, London SW1W 0BS
071-630 1966

NEWSPAPERS

If you wish to comment on the way that women's interests are covered, or on how women are portrayed in a particular newspaper, write to the editor of the paper concerned. The *Guardian* is alone among the national dailies in having a separate page for topics of interest to women every day, but many other national and local papers run regular columns or feature sections covering 'women's issues'. If you would like to see greater coverage of women's issues in your favourite newspaper, then write and say so. You may also wish to see a 'female perspective' (however you interpret that) introduced into the coverage of other news or feature stories. Again, let the people who write and edit the papers you read know what you feel.

NETWORKS FOR WOMEN IN MEDIA, AND MEDIA UNIONS WITH WOMEN'S OFFICERS AND/OR EQUALITY OFFICERS

Women's Film, Television and Video Network
79 Wardour Street, London W1V 3PH
071-434 2076

Women in Publishing
c/o 12 Dyott Street, London WC1A 1DF
071-485 5002

Broadcasting and Entertainment Trades Alliance
Mrs Christina Driver, 181-185 Wardour Street, London W1V 4BE
071-735 9068 ext 216

Equity
Christine Payne, Women's Committee, Equity, 8 Harley Street, London W1N 2AB
071-637 9311

National Union of Journalists
Sally Gilbert (Equality Organiser), Acorn House, 314 Gray's Inn Road, London WC1X 8DP
071-278 7916

Sogat '82
Equality Sub-Committee, SOGAT House, 274/288 London Road, Hadleigh, Essex SS7 2DE
0702-554111
Co-ordinates the equality campaigning and monitoring activities of many of the big print unions.

VOLUNTARY AGENCIES

Campaign Against Pornography
96 Dalston Lane, London E8 1NG
071-923 4303
See also page 8.

Campaign Against Pornography and Censorship (CPC)
PO Box 844, London SE5 9QP
071-274 3072
See also page 8.

Campaign for Press and Broadcasting Freedom (CPBF)
The Unity Club, 96 Dalston Lane, London E8 1NG
071-923 3671 Fax 071-923 3672
See also page 9.

Fawcett Society
Media Committee, 46 Harleyford Road, London SE11 5AY
071-587 1287
See also page 17.

Mothers' Union
Media Project, Mary Sumner House, 27 Tufton Street, London SW1P 3RB
See also page 31.

National Alliance of Women's Organisations (NAWO)
Media Action Group, 279-281 Whitechapel Road, London E1 1BY
071-247 7052
See also page 31.

Appendix 11 Women and work

Industrial Society – Pepperell Unit
Robert Hyde House, 48 Bryanston Square, London W1H 7LN
071-262 2041 Fax 071-706 1096
See also page 22.

Low Pay Unit
9 Upper Berkeley Street, London W1H 8BY
071-262 7278
See also page 28.

National Advisory Centre on Careers for Women
Artillery House, Artillery Row, London SW1P 1RT
071-401 2280

National Council for Civil Liberties (Liberty) – Women's Rights Unit
21 Tabard Street, London SE1 4LA
071-403 3888 Fax 071-407 5354
See also page 35.

New Ways to Work
309 Upper Street, London N1 2TY
071-226 4026
See also page 39.

NUPE Women's National Advisory Committee
Civic House, 20 Grand Depot Road, London SE18 6SF
081-854 2244

Trades Union Congress – Women's Officers
Congress House, Great Russell Street, London WC1 3LS
071-636 4030 Fax 071-636 0632
See also page 52.

Women in Enterprise (WE)
St Gabriels House, 24 Laburnham Road, Wakefield, West Yorks WF1 3QS
0924-361789 Fax 0924-382707
See also page 58.

Women in Management
64 Marryat Road, London SW19 5BN
081-944 6332
See also page 58.

Women in Manual Trades
53-54 Featherstone Street, London EC1Y 8RT
071-251 9193

Women Returners' Network
Garden Cottage, Youngsbury, Ware, Herts SG12 0TZ
0920-464337
See also page 59.

Women's Enterprise Development Agency (WEDA)
Aston Science Park, Love Lane, Aston Triangle, Birmingham B7 4BJ
021-359 0981 Fax 021-359 0433
See also page 61.

Women's Legal Defence Fund
29 Great James Street, London WC1N 3ES
071-831 6890 Fax 071-405 7239
See also page 63.

Working Mothers' Association
7 Holloway Road, London N7 8JZ
071-700 5771 Fax 071-700 1105
See also page 66.

Appendix 12 Finding out

JOURNALS AND MAGAZINES

Everywoman
Everywoman Publishing Ltd, 34 Islington Green, London N1 8DU
071-359 5496

Gender and History
c/o Dr Leonore Davidoff, Department of Sociology, University of Essex, Wivenhoe Park, Colchester CO4 3SQ
0206-873333

History Workshop Journal
PO Box 935, London SE17 1PN

Spare Rib
27 Clerkenwell Close, London EC1 0AT
071-253 9792

Trouble and Strife
c/o Norwich Women's Centre, 34 Exchange Street, Norwich NR2 1AX
0603-628130

Women: A Cultural Review
Oxford University Press, Pinkhill House, Southfield Road, Eynsham, Oxford OX8 1JJ
0865-56767

PUBLISHERS

Onlywomen Press
38 Mount Pleasant, London WC1X 0AP
071-837 0596 Fax 071-833 3477

Pandora Press
77-85 Fulham Palace Road, London W6 8JB
081-741 7070 Fax 081-307 4440

Sheba Feminist Publishers
10A Bradbury Street, London N16 8JN
071-254 1950

Virago Press Ltd
20-23 Mandela Street, London NW1 0HQ
071-385 5150

Women's Press Ltd, The
34 Great Sutton Street, London EC1V 0DX
071-251 3007 Fax 071-608 1938

BOOKSHOPS

Many large bookshops now stock a good selection of books on subjects of interest to women, and works by female and/or feminist writers. The following bookshops are specialist suppliers, who carry an exceptionally wide range of books for women. They will also deal with orders by post.

Silver Moon
68 Charing Cross Road, London WC2H 0BB
071-836 0644

Sisterwrite Bookshop
190 Upper Street, London N1 1RQ
071-226 9782

OTHER SPECIALIST SUPPLIERS

Feminist Audio Books (FAB)
52-54 Featherstone Street, London
EC1Y 8RT
071-251 0713
Runs a postal tape library service of book on subjects of interest to women. *See also* page 18.

Letterbox Library
1st Floor, 8 Bradbury Street, London
N16 8JN
071-254 1540
A book club, selling books by post. Specialises in non-sexist, non-racist books for children and parents. *See also* page 26.

Appendix 13 Organisations which can help you set up a new group

The following organisations may be able to help you with advice and information about setting up a new voluntary organisation to meet your local needs. They may also produce useful publications for sale:

Action Resource Centre
First floor, 102 Park Village East, London NW1 3SP
071-383 2200

Charities Advisory Trust
Radius Works, Back Lane, London NW3 1HL
071-794 9835

Charities Aid Foundation
48 Pembury Road, Tonbridge, Kent TN9 2JD
0732-771333 Fax 0732-350570

Charity Commission
St Alban's House, 57-60 Haymarket, London SW1Y 4QX
071-210 3000 Fax 071-930 9173

National Association of Councils for Voluntary Service
PO Box 717, Sheffield S1 1NL
0742-786636

Directory of Social Change
Radius Works, Back Lane, London NW3 1HL
071-435 8171

Inter-Action Trust
Royal Victoria Dock, London E16 1BT
071-511 0411

National Council for Voluntary Organisations
26 Bedford Square, London WC1B 3HU
071-636 4066 Fax 071-436 3188

National Federation of Community Organisations
8-9 Upper Street, London N1 0PQ
071-226 0189

National Federation of Self-Help Organisations
150 Townmead Road, London SW6 2RA
071-731 8440

Volunteer Centre
29 Lower King's Road, Berkhamstead, Herts HP4 2AB
0442-873311 Fax 0442-870852

It might also be worth writing to organisations listed in this directory (remember to enclose an SAE) who appear to share some of your own aims and objectives, to see whether they have any useful tips to pass on.

Form for new directory entries

If you would like your organisation to be considered for inclusion in the next edition of this directory, please complete the form below and return it, or a photocopy, to: The Editor, Bedford Square Press/NCVO, 26 Bedford Square, London WC1B 3HU.

1. Full name of organisation _____

2. Abbreviated name or acronym if used _____
3. Address of organisation (**including full postal code**)
   _____

4. Telephone number of organisation (**including dialling code**; for London numbers use new codes)
   _____

5. Fax number (for London numbers use new codes)
   _____

6. Full name of one person to contact
   _____

7. BRIEF (no more than 50 words) description of the services/information/advice your organisation can offer to WOMEN. (NB We do NOT need a complete account of the full range of services your organisation can provide.) Longer entries may be cut at the editor's discretion.
   _____
   _____
   _____
   _____
   _____

8. Is your organisation a charity?   Yes/No
9. Do you have branches or local groups?   Yes/No
10. Do you use volunteers in your work?   Yes/No
11. Do you use young volunteers (under 18)?   Yes/No
12. Total number of existing members _____
13. Total number of paid staff _____
14. Do you have a library or information room?   Yes/No
15. Do you have an associated trading company?   Yes/No
    If so, under what name? _____
16. Do you produce publications?   Yes/No
17. Are you a member of NCVO?   Yes/No

I declare that the above information is correct and authorise its inclusion in the next edition of THE WOMEN'S DIRECTORY.
I understand the entry is free.

Signed _____ Date _____
Position _____

If you want to order a copy of the directory, please put tick in box and we will send you a pro forma invoice when the price is known. ☐

Bedford Square Press/NCVO give permission for the above form to be photocopied.

Classified index

ABDUCTED CHILDREN
Portia Trust
National Council for Abducted Children (REUNITE)

ABORTION
Abortion Law Reform Association (ALRA)
Birth Control Campaign
British Pregnancy Advisory Service
Life Care Housing Trust
National Abortion Campagin
Pregnancy Advisory Service
Pro-Choice Alliance
See also Anti-abortion

ACTIVE BIRTH
See Pregnancy/childbirth

ACUPUNCTURE
Women's Natural Health Centre

ADDICTIONS
See Alcohol problems; Drug addiction; Gambling; Tranquiliser overuse

ADOPTION AND FOSTERING
Lesbian and Gay Fostering and Adoptive Parents Network

ADVICE AND INFORMATION SERVICES
Afro-Caribbean Educational Project – Women's Centre
Agorophobia Information Centre
Bangladesh Women's Association in Great Britain
Beaumont Society
British Association for Betterment of Infertility and Education (BABLE)
Brittle Bone Society
Capital Helpline Services
Child
Christian Women's Information and Resources (CWIRES)
Cystitis and Candida
Drugs, Alcohol, Women, Now (DAWN)
Day Care Trust/National Childcare Campaign Ltd
Eating Disorders Association
Endometriosis Association
FAEERU (Women's Group)
Feed-Back
Foundation for Women's Health, Research and Development (FORWARD)
Gay Switchboard
Gay and Lesbian Legal Advice (GLAD)
Infertility Advisory Centre Research Foundation
King's Cross Women's Centre
Latin-American Women's Rights Service
Lesbian and Gay Youth Movement (LGYM)
Lesbian Information Service (LIS)
Lesbian Line
London Irish Women's Centre
London Lesbian and Gay Switchboard
London Lesbian Line (LLL)
Marie Stopes House
Midwives Information and Resource Service (MIDIRS)
NAPS National Headquarters (National Association for Premenstrual Syndrome)
National Association of Citizens Advice Bureaux (NACAB)
National Council for One-Parent Families

National Debtline
National Federation of Community Organisations (NFCO)
National Friend (FRIEND)
National Osteoporosis Society
National Rett Syndrome Association
National Rubella Council
Phobics Society
Prisoners Advice and Information Network (PAIN)
Prisoners Wives and Families Society
Sangam Association for Asian Women
Society to Support Home Confinements
Streetwise Youth Project
Women's Aid Federation (England)
Women's Centre (Northern Ireland Women's Rights Movement)
Women's Corona Society
Women's Employment Enterprise and Training Unit (WEETU)
Women's Health and Reproductive Rights Information Centre
Women's Health Concern
Women's Health Network
Women's Nutritional Advisory Service
Working Mothers Association
Working for Childcare/Workplace Nurseries
See also Conselling; Legal advice; Resource centres/libraries

ADVOCACY

National Citizen Advocacy

AFRICAN AND AFRO-CARIBBEAN ORGANISATIONS

Afro-Caribbean Educational Project – Women's Centre
Foundation for Women's Health, Research and Development (FORWARD)
National Alliance for Women of African Descent
West Indian Women's Association

AFTER-SCHOOL CARE

See Out-of-school care

AGORAPHOBIA

See Phobias

AGRICULTURE

Farm Women's Club
Women's Farm and Garden Association
Women's Farming Union

AIDS

Catholic AIDS Link
London Lesbian and Gay Switchboard
National Abortion Campaign
PACE (Project for Advice, Counselling and Information)
Positively Women

ALCOHOL PROBLEMS

Al-Anon Family Groups
Alcohol Counselling Service
Alcoholics Anonymous (AA)
Drugs, Alcohol, Women, Now (DAWN)
National British Women's Total Abstinence Union
Women's Alcohol Centre

ALTERNATIVE MEDICINE

See Complementary medicine

ANOREXIA/BULIMIA NERVOSA

Anorexics Anonymous
Eating Disorders Association
Feed-Back
Overeaters Anonymous
SARA (Society for the Advancement of Research into Anorexia)
Spare Tyre

ANTE-NATAL CLASSES

See Pregnancy/childbirth

ANTI-ABORTION

LIFE (Save the Unborn Child)
Society for the Protection of Unborn Children
See also Abortion

ANTI-FEMINISM

Concern for Family and Womanhood
  – Campaign for the Feminine
  Woman
See also Feminism

ARMS/DISARMAMENT

Black Women for Wages for
  Housework
NATO Alerts Network

ART THERAPY

PACE (Project for Advice, Counselling
  and Information)

ARTIFICIAL INSEMINATION

See Infertility

ARTS/CRAFTS

Aphra Videos
Cinema of Women (COW)
Embroiderers' Guild
Gay Authors Workshop
Knitting and Crochet Guild
Lace Guild
National Federation of Women's
  Institutes (NFWI)
Pascal Theatre Company
Quilters Guild
Radclyffe Hall Memorial Fund
Royal School of Needlework
South-West Women's Arts Network
  (SWWAN)
Spare Tyre
United Kingdom Home Economics
  Federation
Women Artists' Slide Library
See also Drama; Film; Museums

ASIANS

Asian Young Women's Project
  (AYWP)
Bangladesh Women's Association in
  Great Britain
Sangam Association for Asian
  Women
See also Ethnic minorities

ASSERTIVENESS

Industrial Society, Pepperell Unit
Redwood Women's Training
  Association
Women in Training

AU PAIRS

International Catholic Society for Girls
  (ACISJF)

BABIES: CRYING

CRY-SIS Support Group

BABIES: PREMATURE

BLISS (Baby Life Support Systems)
National Information for Parents of
  Prematures: Education, Research
  and Support (NIPPERS)

'BABY BLUES'

See Post-natal depression

BABY SNATCHING

See Abducted children

BATTERED WOMEN

See Domestic violence

BENEFITS

See Welfare rights/benefits

BENEVOLENT ASSOCIATIONS

Queen's Nursing Institute
Royal British Legion Women's Section
Schoolmistresses and Governesses
  Benevolent Institution

BEREAVEMENT

Cruse — Bereavement Care
Foundation for the Study of Infant
  Deaths
Gay Bereavement Project
Twins and Multiple Births
  Association

BIRTH CONTROL

Birth Control Campaign
Birth Control Trust
British Pregnancy Advisory Service
Brook Advisory Centres
Copper 7 Association
Dalkon Shield Association
Family Planning Association
International Planned Parenthood Federation
Marie Stopes House
National Association of Natural Family Planning Teachers
Pregnancy Advisory Service

BIRTH DEFECTS

Foresight Charity for Preconceptual Care
National Rubella Council
PROGRESS (Campaign for Research into Human Reproduction)
Toxoplasmosis Trust

BLINDNESS/VISUAL HANDICAP

Feminist Audio Books (FAB)
Women's Tapeover

BOWEL DISEASE

Genetic Clinic

BREAST CARE

Breast Cancer Research Trust
Breast Care and Mastectomy Association
Genetic Clinic
Women's National Cancer Control Campaign

BREASTFEEDING

Association of Breastfeeding Mothers
Baby Milk Action
La Leche League
National Childbirth Trust (NCT)

BRITTLE BONE DISEASE

Brittle Bone Society

BULIMIA NERVOSA

See Anorexia/bulimia nervosa

BUSINESSWOMEN

British Association of Women Enterpreneurs (BAWE)
City Women's Network
Women in Enterprise
Women into Business
Women's Enterprise Development Agency

CAESARIAN DELIVERIES

Caesarian Support Group of Cambridge
National Childbirth Trust (NCT)

CAMPAIGNING/LOBBYING

35's Women's Campaign for Soviet Jewry
300 Group
Abortion Law Reform Association (ALRA)
Birth Control Campaign
Black Women for Wages for Housework
Campaign Against Pornography
Campaign Against Pornography and Censorship (CPC)
Campaign for Homosexual Equality (CHE)
Child Poverty Action Group (CPAG)
Copper 7 Association
Elizabeth Garrett Anderson Action Committee
English Collective of Prostitutes (ECP)
King's Cross Women's Centre
Lesbian and Gay Youth Movement (LGYM)
LIFE (Save the Unborn Child)
Low Pay Unit
Married Women's Association
Maternity Alliance
National Abortion Campaign
National Alliance of Women's Organisations
National Campaign for Nursery Education

National Council for One-Parent Families
National Housewives Association (NHA)
National Joint Committee of Working Women's Organisations
Pro-Choice Alliance
Society for the Protection of Unborn Children
Stonewall Lobby Group Ltd
United Kingdom Federation of Business and Professional Women (BPW)
VDU Workers' Rights Campaign
Wages for Housework Campaign
We Welcome Small Children National Campaign
WinVisible (Women with Visible and Invisible Disabilities)
Women Against Sexual Harassment (WASH)

CANCER

Breast Cancer Research Trust
Breast Care and Mastectomy Association
Family Cancer Clinic
Genetic Clinic
Helene Harris Memorial Trust
Women's National Cancer Control Campaign

CAREER BREAKS

See Return to work

CAREERS

Academic Women's Achievement Group
Association of Women Solicitors (1919 Club)
Careers for Women
City Women's Network
HERA for Women (Housing Employment Register and Advice)
Industrial Society, Pepperell Unit
Law Society Women's Careers Working Party
Medical Women's Federation
National Association of Women Pharmacists
National Organisation for Women's Management Education (NOWME)
Open University Women into Science and Engineering (WISE) Group
Royal College of Midwives Trust
Royal College of Nursing
Women and Manual Trades (WAMT)
Women in Enterprise
Women in Management
Women in Publishing
Women into Business
Women's Engineering Society
Women's Enterprise Development Agency
Women's Farm and Garden Association
See also Education and training; Employment

CARERS/CARE SCHEMES

Break
Women's Royal Voluntary Service

CATHOLIC CHURCH ORGANISATIONS

Catholic AIDS Link
Catholic Marriage Advisory Council
Catholic Needlework Guild (CNG)
Catholic Women's League
International Catholic Society for Girls (ACISJF)
National Board of Catholic Women (NBCW)
Roman Catholic Feminists
Union of Catholic Mothers of England and Wales

CENSORSHIP

Campaign Against Pornography and Censorship (CPC)

CERVICAL STITCH

Cervical Stitch Network

CHILD ABUSE

Lifeline – Help for Victims of Violence in the Home

National Society for the Prevention of Cruelty to Children (NSPCC)
Ormiston Trust
PAIN (Parents Against INjustice)

CHILD CUSTODY

Legal Action for Women (LAW)
Wages Due Lesbians

CHILDBIRTH

See Pregnancy/childbirth

CHILDLESSNESS

British Organisation of Non-Parents (BON)
National Association for the Childless
See also Infertility

CHILDREN/CHILD CARE

British Association for Neighbourhood Daycare
Child Poverty Action Group
Day Care Trust/National Childcare Campaign Ltd
Families Need Fathers
National Association for Maternal and Child Welfare
National Campaign for Nursery Education
National Childminding Association
National Housewives Association (NHA)
National Society for the Prevention of Cruelty to Children (NSPCC)
Ormiston Trust
Practical Alternatives for Mums, Dads and Under-Fives (PRAM)
We Welcome Small Children National Campaign
Working Mothers Association
Working for Childcare/Workplace Nurseries
See also Abducted children; Child custody; Family support and welfare; Pre-school children

CHRISTIAN ORGANISATIONS

Girls Brigade
Girls Friendly Society and Townsend Fellowship
Institute for the Study of Christianity and Sexuality
Lesbian and Gay Christian Movement
Mothers' Union
Movement for the Ordination of Women
National Free Church Women's Council
Student Christian Movement Women's Network
Women's Inter-Church Consultative Committee
Young Women's Christian Association of Great Britain (YWCA)
See also Catholic church organisations; Religious organisations

CLUBS

See Social/cultural activities

COMMUNITY DEVELOPMENT

National Federation of Community Organisations (NFCO)
National Federation of Self-Help Organisations
Soroptimist International of Great Britain and Ireland

COMMUNITY SERVICE

See Volunteering/community service

COMPLEMENTARY MEDICINE

Vineyard Project
Women's Natural Health Centre

COMPUTERS

City Centre
Microsyster
VDU Workers' Rights Campaign

CONCILIATION SERVICES

Divorce Conciliation Advisory Service
National Family Conciliation Council

CONGENITAL ABNORMALITIES

See Birth defects

CONSERVATION

See Environment/conservation

CONSUMER AFFAIRS

Townswomen's Guild
We Welcome Small Children National Campaign
Women's Farming Union
Women's Gas Federation

CONTRACEPTION

See Birth control

CO-OPERATIVES

Co-operative Women's Guild

CO-ORDINATING/UMBRELLA BODIES

National Alliance of Women's Organisations
National Assembly of Women
National Council of Women of Great Britain
National Federation of Community Organisations (NFCO)
National Federation of Self-Help Organisations
Standing Conference of Women's Organisations
Women's National Commission

COT DEATH

Foundation for the Study of Infant Deaths

COUNSELLING

Alcohol Counselling Service
Anorexics Anonymous
Association for Post-Natal Illness
Beaumont Society
British Association for Betterment of Infertility and Education (BABLE)
Brook Advisory Centres
Capital Helpline Services
Catholic Marriage Advisory Council
CHAT
Child
Crisis Counselling for Alleged Shoplifters
Cruse – Bereavement Care
Cystitis and Candida
Divorce Conciliation Advisory Service
Exploring Parenthood
Feed-Back
Foundation for Women's Health, Research and Development (Forward)
Gender Dysphoria Trust (GDT)
Identity
Infertility Advisory Centre Research Foundation
Institute for the Study of Christianity and Sexuality
LIFE (Save the Unborn Child)
Life Care and Housing Trust
Lifeline – Help for Victims of Violence in the Home
London Friend
London Lesbian and Gay Centre
London Lesbian and Gay Switchboard
Meet-a-Mum Association (MAMA)
National Friend (FRIEND)
One Plus One (Marriage and Partnership Research)
PACE (Project for Advice, Counselling and Information)
Phobics Society
Positively Women
Pregnancy Advisory Service
Prisoners Wives and Families Society
Rape Crisis Centre
Relate (National Marriage Guidance)
Samaritans
SPOD (Association to Aid the Sexual and Personal Relationships of People with a Disability)
Stepfamily
Streetwise Youth Project
Women's Alcohol Centre
Women's Health Information and Support Centre
Women's Therapy Centre
See also Emotional problems; Mental health and illness

CRAFTS
See Arts/crafts

CRYING BABIES
See Babies: crying

CULTURAL ACTIVITIES
See Social/cultural activities

CULTURAL LINKS BETWEEN COUNTRIES
Associated Country Women of the World
British Federation of University Women
Chile Solidarity Campaign Women's Section
European Forum of Socialist Feminists - UK Group
Singapore and Malaysian British Association (SIMBA) (Women's Section)
Soroptimist International of Great Britain and Ireland
Union of Turkish Women in Britain (UTWB)
Women Welcome Women
Women's Corona Society
See also International co-operation; Social/cultural activities

CYPRIOTS
Cypriot Women's League

CYSTITIS
Cystitis and Candida

DEBT/MONEY MANAGEMENT
Money Management Council
National Debtline

DEPRESSION
Identity
Phobics Society
Portia Trust
Samaritans

See also Counselling; Emotional problems; Mental health and illness; Post-natal depression; Psychotherapy

DEVELOPING COUNTRIES
See International aid organisations

DEVELOPMENT EDUCATION
Women's Development Agency (ADVO WDA)
Womankind (Worldwide)

DIET
See Nutrition/diet

DIETING
See Weight problems

DISABILITY
Break
Brothers and Sisters Club
Feminist Audio Books (FAB)
Gemma
Parents with Disabilities Group
SPOD (Association to Aid the Sexual and Personal Relationships of People with a Disability)
WinVisible (Women with Visible and Invisible Disabilities)
Women's Tapeover

DIVORCE AND SEPARATION
Divorce Conciliation Advisory Service
Families Need Fathers
National Council for the Divorced and Separated
National Family Conciliation Council

DOMESTIC VIOLENCE
Black Women for Wages for Housework
Chiswick Family Rescue
King's Cross Women's Centre
Legal Action for Women (LAW)
Lifeline - Help for Victims of Violence in the Home

Rape Crisis Centre
Women Against Rape
Women's Aid Federation (England)
See also Child abuse

DRAMA

Pascal Theatre Company
Spare Tyre

DRINKING

See Alcohol problems

DRUG ADDICTION/SIDE-EFFECTS

Drugs, Alcohol, Women, Now (DAWN)
Steroid Aid Group
Vineyard Project

DUKE OF EDINBURGH AWARDS

Girls Brigade
Girls Venture Corps Air Cadets

EATING DISORDERS

See Anorexia/bulimia nervosa; Weight problems

ECOLOGY

See Environment/conservation

EDUCATION AND TRAINING

Academic Women's Achievement Group
Afro-Caribbean Educational Project – Women's Centre
Associated Country Women of the World
British Federation of University Women
Centre for Women's Studies
Creative and Supportive Trust (CAST)
CREW
Girls' Public Day School Trust
Girls' Schools Association
HERA for Women (Housing Employment Register and Advice)
Industrial Society, Pepperell Unit
Local Education Authorities Equal Opportunities Consortium (LEAC)
Milton Keynes Women and Work Group
National Association of Women's Clubs
National Federation of Community Organisations (NFCO)
National Federation of Women's Institutes (NFWI)
Open University Women into Science and Engineering (WISE) Group
Reading Women's Education Project Ltd
Redwood Women's Training Association
Suzy Lamplugh Trust
Townswomen's Guilds
West Indian Women's Association
Women and Training
Women in Education: The National Association
Women in Training
Women Returners' Network
Women's Development Agency (ADVO WDA)
Women's Employment Enterprise and Training Unit (WEETU)
See also Careers; Employment

EMBRYO RESEARCH

LIFE (Save the Unborn Child)
PROGRESS (Campaign for Research into Human Reproduction)

EMERGENCY RELIEF: OVERSEAS

Catholic Needlework Guild (CNG)
Catholic Women's League
See also International aid organisations

EMERGENCY RELIEF: UK

Women's Royal Voluntary Service

EMOTIONAL PROBLEMS

Association for Post-Natal Illness
Brook Advisory Centres
Identity
Meet-a-Mum Association (MAMA)
Network for Supporting Children of People with Mental Distress (NSCPMD)

Open Door Association
Portia Trust
Samaritans
Women's Therapy Centre
See also Counselling; Mental health and illness; Psychotherapy

EMPLOYMENT RIGHTS

City Centre
Lesbian and Gay Employment Rights (LAGER)
Low Pay Unit
Maternity Alliance
National Homeworking Unit
National Joint Committee or Working Women's Organisations
Trades Union Congress
VDU Workers' Rights Campaign
Women Against Sexual Harassment (WASH)
Working Mothers Association

EMPLOYMENT/UNEMPLOYMENT

British Association of Women Entrepreneurs (BAWE)
Careers for Women
Centre for Women's Studies

Creative and Supportive Trust (CAST)
CREW
HERA for Women (Housing Employment Register and Advice)
Industrial Society, Pepperell Unit
Low Pay Unit
Milton Keynes Women and Work Group
National Homeworking Unit
National Joint Committee of Working Women's Organisations
National Organisation for Women's Management Education (NOWME)
New Ways to Work
Reading Women's Education Project Ltd
Women and Manual Trades (WAMT)
Women in Enterprise
Women in Management
Women in Publishing
Women in Training
Women into Business

Women Returners' Network
Women Working Worldwide
Women's Employment Enterprise and Training Unit (WEETU)
Women's Engineering Society
Working Mothers Association
Working for Childcare/Workplace Nurseries

ENDOMETRIOSIS

Endometriosis Society

ENGINEERING

Open University Women into Science and Engineering (WISE) Group
Women's Engineering Society

ENVIRONMENT/CONSERVATION

Black Women for Wages for Housework
Townswomen's Guilds

ENVIRONMENTAL HEALTH

City Centre
Foresight Charity for Preconceptual Care
VDU Workers' Rights Campaign
Work Injured Nurses Group (WING)

EQUAL OPPORTUNITIES

Baha'i National Women's Committee
City Centre
Fawcett Society
Industrial Society, Pepperell Unit
Josephine Butler Society
Local Education Authorities Equal Opportunities Consortium (LEAC)
Married Women's Association
Medical Women's Federation
National Alliance of Women's Organisations
National Assembly of Women
National Association of Local Government Women's Committees
New Ways to Work
Sex, Race and Class (Black and Third World Women's Discussion and Study Group) (SRC)

Time Off for Women
Trades Union Congress
United Kingdom Federation of
  Business and Professional Women
  (BPW)
Women, Heritage and Museums
Women in Education: The National
  Association
Women's Legal Defence Fund
Women's Resource Centre
Women's Sports Foundation (WSF)
See also Racism; Sex discrimination

ETHNIC MINORITIES

Afro-Caribbean Education Project –
  Women's Centre
Bangladesh Women's Association in
  Great Britain
Black Female Prisoners Scheme
Black Women for Wages for
  Housework
Cypriot Women's League
FAEERU (Women's Group)
Foundation for Women's Health,
  Research and Development
  (FORWARD)
Latin-American Women's Rights
  Service
League of Jewish Women
London Black Women's Health Action
  Project
London Irish Women's Centre
Maternity Links
Maternity Services Liaison Scheme
National Alliance for Women of
  African Descent
National Federation of Self-Help
  Organisations
National Self-Help Support Networks
Sangam Association for Asian
  Women
Sex, Race and Class (Black and Third
  World Women's Discussion and
  Study Group (SRC)
Union of Turkish Women in Britain
  (UTWB)
Women's Centre (Northern Ireland
  Women's Rights Movement)
Women's Development Agency
  (ADVO WDA)

EUROPE

CREW
European Forum of Socialist
  Feminists – UK Group
National Alliance of Women's
  Organisations

EXCHANGE PROGRAMMES

Associated Country Women of the
  World
Women Welcome Women

FAMILY PLANNING

See Birth control

FAMILY SUPPORT AND WELFARE

Bangladesh Women's Association of
  Great Britain
British Housewives League
Catholic Marriage Advisory Council
Child Poverty Action Group
CRY-SIS Support Group
Exploring Parenthood
Gingerbread
HALOW (Help and Advice Line for
  Offenders' Wives)
Lifeline – Help for Victims of Violence
  in the Home
Mothers' Union
Multiple Births Foundation
National Association for Maternal and
  Child Welfare
National Council for One-Parent
  Families
National Society for the Prevention of
  Cruelty to Children (NSPCC)
Network for Supporting Children of
  People with Mental Distress
  (NSCPMD)
One Plus One (Marriage and
  Partnership Research)
Ormiston Trust
PAIN (Parents Against INjustice)
Parent Network
Parents Anonymous (London)
Relate (National Marriage Guidance)
Salvation Army Investigation
  Department
Stepfamily

Twins and Multiple Birth Association
Union of Catholic Mothers of England and Wales
See also Children/child care; Marriage counselling

FEMALE CIRCUMCISION

Foundation for Women's Health, Research and Development (FORWARD)
London Black Women's Health Action Project

FEMINISM

Christian Women's Information and Resources (CWIRES)
European Forum of Socialist Feminists – UK Group
Feminist Archive
Feminist Library
Older Feminist Network
Roman Catholic Feminists
Student Christian Movement Women's Network
See also Anti-feminism

FERTILITY PROBLEMS

See Infertility

FILM

Aphra Videos
Cinema of Women (COW)
Women's Media Resource Project
See also Media

FLEXIBLE WORKING

New Ways to Work

FOSTERING

See Adoption and fostering

GAMBLING

National British Women's Total Abstinence Union

GARDENING/HORTICULTURE

Women's Farm and Garden Association

GAYS/LESBIANS

Brothers and Sisters Club
Campaign for Homosexual Equality (CHE)
Gay and Lesbian Legal Advice (GLAD)
Gay Authors Workshop
Gay Bereavement Project
Gay Switchboard
Gemma
Kenric
Lesbian and Gay Christian Movement
Lesbian and Gay Employment Rights (LAGER)
Lesbian and Gay Fostering and Adoptive Parents Network
Lesbian and Gay Pride Organising Committee
Lesbian and Gay Youth Movement (LGYM)
Lesbian Archive and Information Centre (LAIC)
Lesbian Information Service (LIS)
Lesbian Line
London Friend
London Lesbian and Gay Centre
London Lesbian and Gay Switchboard
London Lesbian Line
Mature Lesbian Group
National Friend (FRIEND)
PACE (Project for Advice, Counselling and Information)
Stonewall Lobby Group Ltd
Wages Due Lesbians

GERMAN MEASLES

See Rubella

GIRLS

See Young people

GUIDES

Girl Guides Association
Scout and Guide Graduate Association (SAGGA)

HANDICAP

See Disability

HEALING
Women's Natural Health Centre

HEALTH AND MEDICINE
Foresight Charity for Preconceptual Care
Health Rights
Herpes Association
International Planned Parenthood Federation
Medical Women's Federation
Open Door Association
Royal College of Midwives Trust
Royal College of Nursing
See also Complementary medicine; Environmental health; Mental health and illness; Women: health

HEALTH AND MEDICINE: OVERSEAS
Chile Solidarity Campaign Women's Section
Womankind (Worldwide)

HEALTH AND SAFETY
See Environmental health

HERBALISM
Women's Natural Health Centre

HERPES
Herpes Association

HISTORY
Fawcett Library
Feminist Archive
Lesbian Archive and Information Centre (LAIC)
Pankhurst Trust
Radclyffe Hall Memorial Fund
Women, Heritage and Museums
Women in Economic and Social History

HIV (HUMAN IMMUNODEFICIENCY VIRUS)
See AIDS

HOLIDAYS
Break
Holidays One-Parents (HOP)
One-Parent Family Holidays (OPF Holidays)
SPLASH (Single Parent Links and Special Holidays)
Women's Holiday Centre

HOME ECONOMICS
United Kingdom Home Economics Federation

HOMELESSNESS
Girls Alone Project (GAP)
Life Care and Housing Trust
See also Housing

HOMEOPATHY
Women's Natural Health Centre

HOMEWORKERS
Cypriot Women's League
National Homeworking Unit

HORMONE REPLACEMENT THERAPY
Women's Health Concern

HOUSEWIVES
Associated Country Women of the World
British Housewives League
Concern for Family and Womanhood Campaign for the Feminine Woman
National Housewives Association (NHA)

HOUSING/ACCOMMODATION
Catholic Women's League
Housing Link for Women
Life Care and Housing Trust
National Free Church Women's Council
One-Parent Housing
Over Forty Association for Women Workers

United Kingdom Federation of Business and Professional Women (BPW)
Young Women's Christian Association of Great Britain (YWCA)
See also Homelessness

HUMAN RIGHTS

35's Women's Campaign for Soviet Jewry
Chile Solidarity Campaign Women's Section
Singapore and Malaysian British Association (SIMBA) (Women's Section)
Union of Turkish Women in Britain (UTWB)
See also Censorship; Law and justice

HYSTERECTOMY

Hysterectomy Support Group (HSG)

IMMIGRATION

Bangladesh Women's Association in Great Britain
FAEERU (Women's Group)
Legal Action for Women (LAW)
Sangam Association for Asian Women

INCEST

Asian Young Women's Project (AYWP)
Rape Crisis Centre

INFERTILITY

British Association for Betterment of Infertility and Education (BABLE)
British Pregnancy Advisory Service
Child
Endometriosis Society
Infertility Advisory Centre Research Foundation
Life Care and Housing Trust
National Association for the Childless
Pregnancy Advisory Service
PROGRESS (Campaign for Research into Human Reproduction)

INFORMATION SERVICES

See Advice and information services; Resource centres/libraries

INTERNATIONAL AID ORGANISATIONS

Catholic Needlework Guild (CNG)
Catholic Women's League
Chile Solidarity Campaign Women's Section
Womankind (Worldwide)
Women's Development Agency (ADVO WDA)
See also Poverty: overseas

INTERNATIONAL CO-OPERATION

Associated Country Women of the World
Change
European Forum of Socialist Feminists – UK Group
International Catholic Society for Girls (ACISJF)
National Women's Network for International Solidarity
Soroptimist International of Great Britain and Ireland
Time Off for Women
United Kingdom Federation of Business and Professional Women (BPW)
Wages for Housework Campaign
Womankind (Worldwide)
Women Welcome Women
Women Working Worldwide
Women's Corona Society
Women's International League for Peace and Freedom
See also Cultural links between countries

INTERPRETATION AND TRANSLATION

Maternity Links
Maternity Services Liaison Scheme
Union of Turkish Women in Britain (UTWB)

IRISH ORGANISATIONS

London Irish Women's Centre
Women's Centre (Northern Ireland Women's Rights Movement)

JEWISH ORGANISATIONS

35's Women's Campaign for Soviet Jewry
League of Jewish Women

JOB SHARING

See Flexible working

JUSTICE

See Law and Justice

LADIES' CIRCLES

National Association of Ladies' Circles of Great Britain and Ireland

LATIN AMERICANS

Chile Solidarity Campaign Women's Section
FAEERU (Women's Group)
Latin-American Women's Rights Service

LAW AND JUSTICE

Gay and Lesbian Legal Advice (GLAD)
Josephine Butler Society
Legal Action for Women (LAW)
National Citizen Advocacy
Peace House
Rights of Women
Women's Legal Defence Fund

LEGAL ADVICE

Copper 7 Association
Dalkon Shield Association
Gay and Lesbian Legal Advice (GLAD)
King's Cross Women's Centre
Legal Action for Women (LAW)
London Lesbian and Gay Switchboard
National Association of Citizens Advice Bureau (NACAB)
National Citizen Advocacy
National Debtline
Prisoners Wives and Families Society
Rape Crisis Centre
Rights of Women
Society for the Protection of Unborn Children
Streetwise Youth Project
Women Against Sexual Harassment (WASH)
Women's Legal Defence Fund

LESBIANS

See Gays/lesbians

LIBRARIES

See Resource centres/libraries

LOBBYING

See Campaigning/lobbying

LOCAL GOVERNMENT

National Association of Local Government Women's Committees

LONELINESS/ISOLATION

Kenric
Meet-a-Mum Association (MAMA)
Portia Trust
Vineyard Project

MANAGEMENT

Industrial Society, Pepperell Unit
National Organisation for Women's Management Education (NOWME)
Women in Management
Women in Training
Women's Enterprise Development Agency

MANUAL TRADES

Reading Women's Education Project Ltd
Women and Manual Trades (WAMT)

MARRIAGE COUNSELLING

Catholic Marriage Advisory Council

Married Women's Association
One Plus One (Marriage and Partnership Research)
Relate (National Marriage Guidance)

MASTECTOMY

Breast Cancer and Mastectomy Association

MATERNITY SERVICES

See Pregnancy/childbirth

MEDIA

Aphra Videos
Cinema of Women (COW)
Women and the Media
Women's Media Resource Project

MENOPAUSE

Women's Health Concern
Women's Nutritional Advisory Service

MENTAL HEALTH AND ILLNESS

Association for Post-Natal Illness
Meet-a-Mum Association (MAMA)
Network for Supporting Children of People with Mental Distress (NSCPMD)
Open Door Association
Phobics Society
Samaritans
Women's Therapy Centre
See also Emotional problems

MIDWIVES

Midwives Information and Resource Service (MIDIRS)
Royal College of Midwives Trust

MINORITY GROUPS

See Ethnic minorities

MISCARRIAGE

Cervical Stitch Network
Miscarriage Association
National Childbirth Trust (NCT)

PROGRESS (Campaign for Research into Human Reproduction)

MISSING PERSONS/RUNAWAYS

Salvation Army Investigation Department
Suzy Lamplugh Trust

MONEY MANAGEMENT

See Debt/money management

MORALITY

Josephine Butler Society
National British Women's Total Abstinence Union
National Free Church Women's Council

MOTHERS

Association of Breastfeeding Mothers
La Leche League (GB)
MATCH (Mothers Apart from their Children)
Meet-a-Mum Association (MAMA)
Mothers' Union
National Association for Maternal and Child Welfare
Trust for the Study of Adolescence
Working Mothers Association
Working for Childcare/Workplace Nurseries
See also Parenthood

MUTIPLE BIRTHS

See Twins/multiple births

MUSEUMS

Women, Heritage and Museums

NEW TECHNOLOGY

See Computers

NUCLEAR DISARMAMENT

See Arms/disarmament

NURSERIES

See Pre-school children

NURSING
CHAT
Queen's Nursing Institute
Royal College of Nursing
Work Injured Nurses Group (WING)

NUTRITION/DIET
Women's Nutritional Advisory Service

OBESITY
See Weight problems

OFFENDERS' FAMILIES
HALOW (Help and Advice Line for Offenders' Wives)
Prisoners Advice and Information Network (PAIN)
Prisoners Wives and Families Society

OFFENDERS/EX-OFFENDERS
Black Female Prisoners Scheme
Creative and Supportive Trust (CAST)
Prisoners Advice and Information Network (PAIN)

OLDER WOMEN
Housing Link for Women
Mature Lesbian Group
Older Feminist Network
Over Forty Association for Women Workers

ONE-PARENT FAMILIES
Gingerbread
Holidays One-Parents (HOP)
Life Care and Housing Trust
National Council for One-Parent Families
One-Parent Family Holidays (OPF Holidays)
One-Parent Housing
SPLASH (Single Parent Links and Special Holidays)
See also Family support and welfare

ORDINATION OF WOMEN
Movement for the Ordination of Women

OSTEOPATHY
Women's Natural Health Centre

OSTEOPOROSIS
National Osteoporosis Society
Women's Health Concern

OUT-OF-SCHOOL CARE
Bristol Association for Neighbourhood Daycare
Day Care Trust/National Childcare Campaign Ltd
National Childminding Association
West Indian Women's Association
Working Women's Association

OVERSEAS AID/DEVELOPMENT
See International aid organisations

PARENTHOOD
Association for Improvements in the Maternity Services (AIMS)
Baby Milk Action
British Organisation of Non-Parents (BON)
CRY-SIS Support Group
Day Care Trust/National Childcare Campaign Ltd
Exploring Parenthood
Foresight Charity for Preconceptual Care
International Planned Parenthood Federation
Lesbian and Gay Fostering and Adoptive Parents Network
MATCH (Mothers Apart from their Children)
Mothers' Union
Multiple Births Foundation
National Association for Maternal and Child Welfare
National Childbirth Trust
National Information for Parents of Prematures: Education, Resources and Support (NIPPERS)
National Society for the Prevention of Cruelty to Children (NSPCC)
PAIN (Parents Against INjustice)
Parent Network

Parents Anonymous (London)
Parents with Disabilities Group
Trust for the Study of Adolescence
See also Mothers

PATIENTS' RIGHTS/ PARTICIPATION

Copper 7 Association
Dalkon Shield Association
Elizabeth Garrett Anderson Action Committee
Health Rights
National Abortion Campaign

PEACE ORGANISATIONS

Co-operative Women's Guild
National British Women's Total Abstinence Union
Peace House
Women's International League for Peace and Freedom
See also Arms/disarmament

PENFRIENDS

Associated Country Women of the World
Kenric
Lesbian and Gay Youth Movement (LGYM)

PERSONAL DEVELOPMENT

300 Group
Girls' Brigade
Girls Venture Corps Air Cadets
Industrial Society, Pepperell Unit
National Association of Women's Clubs
National Women's Register
Redwood Women's Training Association
Sex, Race and Class (Black and Third World Women's Discussion and Study Group) (SRC)
Suzy Lamplugh Trust
Townswomen's Guilds
Women in Management
Women in Training

PERSONAL RELATIONSHIPS

Catholic Marriage Advisory Council
Identity
Lifeline – Help for Victims of Violence in the Home
One Plus One (Marriage and Partnership Research)
Relate (National Marriage Guidance)
SPOD (Association to Aid the Sexual and Personal Relationships of People with a Disability)
Trust for the Study of Adolescence

PERSONAL SAFETY

Suzy Lamplugh Trust
Women Against Rape
Women for Improved Transport (WIT)
Women's Aid Federation (England)

PHOBIAS

Agoraphobia Information Service
Open Door Association
Phobics Society

PHYSICAL HANDICAP

See Disability

PLAYGROUPS

See Pre-school children

POLITICS

300 Group
Conservative Women's National Committee
European Forum of Socialist Feminists – UK Group
NATO Alerts Network
Shadow Ministry for Women
Women's National Commission
See also Campaigning/lobbying

PORNOGRAPHY

Campaign Against Pornography
Campaign Against Pornography and Censorship

POSITION OF WOMEN IN SOCIETY

300 Group
Associated Country Women of the World
Black Women for Wages for Housework
Change
CREW
European Forum of Socialist Feminists – UK Group
National Alliance of Women's Organisations
National Assembly of Women
National Association of Local Government Women's Committees
National Council of Women of Great Britain
National Women's Network for International Solidarity
Older Feminist Network
Shadow Ministry for Women
Standing Conference of Women's Organisations
United Kingdom Federation of Business and Professional Women (BPW)
Women's National Commission

POST-NATAL DEPRESSION

Association for Post-Natal Illness
Meet-a-Mum Association (MAMA)
NAPS National Headquarters (National Association for Premenstrual Syndrome)

POVERTY: OVERSEAS

Associated Country Women of the World
Catholic Needlework Guild (CNG)
Womankind (Worldwide)
Women's Development Agency (ADVO WDA)

POVERTY: UK

Catholic Needlework Guild (CNG)
Child Poverty Action Group
Low Pay Unit
National Association of Citizens Advice Bureaux (NACAB)
Women's Royal Voluntary Service

PRE-CONCEPTUAL CARE

See Pregnancy/childbirth

PREGNANCY/CHILDBIRTH

Active Birth Centre
Association for Improvements in the Maternity Services (AIMS)
Association for Post-Natal Illness
Birthright
BLISS (Baby Life Support Systems)
British Pregnancy Advisory Service
Caesarian Support Group of Cambridge
Cervical Stitch Network
Foresight Charity for Preconceptual Care
Life Care and Housing Trust
Maternity Alliance
Maternity Links
Maternity Services Liaison Scheme
Midwives Information and Resource Service (MIDIRS)
Miscarriage Association
National Childbirth Trust (NCT)
National Rubella Council
Parents with Disabilities Group
Pregnancy Advisory Service
Royal College of Midwives Trust
Society to Support Home Confinements
Toxoplasmosis Trust

PREMATURE BABIES

See Babies: premature

PRE-MENSTRUAL SYNDROME/TENSION

NAPS National Headquarters (National Association for Premenstrual Syndrome)
Premenstrual Society (PREMSOC)
Women's Nutritional Advisory Service

PRE-SCHOOL CHILDREN

Day Care Trust/National Childcare Campaign Ltd

National Campaign for Nursery Education
National Childminding Association
Practical Alternatives for Mums, Dads and Under-Fives (PRAM)
Pre-School Playgroups Association
We Welcome Small Children National Campaign
Working for Childcare/Workplace Nurseries
Working Mothers Association

PROFESSIONAL WOMEN

Academic Women's Achievement Group
Association of Women Solicitors (1919 Club)
British Association of Women Entrepreneurs (BAWE)
British Federation of University Women
Careers for Women
City Women's Network
Law Society Women's Careers Working Party
Medical Women's Federation
National Association of Women Pharmacists
Open University Women into Science and Engineering (WISE) Group
Rights of Women
Royal College of Midwives Trust
Royal College of Nursing
Soroptimist International of Great Britain and Ireland
United Kingdom Federation of Business and Professional Women (BPW)
Women in Enterprise
Women in Management
Women in Publishing
Women into Business
Women's Engineering Society
Women's Enterprise Development Agency
Women's Farm and Garden Association

PROSTITUTION

Black Women for Wages for Housework
English Collective of Prostitutes (ECP)
King's Cross Women's Centre
Legal Action for Women (LAW)
Streetwise Youth Project

PSYCHIATRIC/PSYCHOLOGICAL PROBLEMS

See Emotional problems; Mental health and illness; Psychotherapy

PSYCHOTHERAPY

Women's Natural Health Centre
Women's Therapy Centre
See also Counselling

PUBLISHING

See Writing/publishing

RACISM/RACE EQUALITY/RACE RELATIONS

Black Women for Wages for Housework
King's Cross Women's Centre
Letterbox Library
Sex, Race and Class (Black and Third World Women's Discussion and Study Group) (SRC)
Time Off for Women
Trades Union Congress
Women's Resource Centre
See also Equal opportunities; Ethnic minorities

RAPE

Black Women for Wages for Housework
Campaign Against Pornography
King's Cross Women's Centre
Legal Action for Women (LAW)
Rape Crisis Centre
Women Against Rape
See also Domestic violence; Incest; Victims of crime

RECREATION/LEISURE

National Federation of Community Organisations (NFCO)
Townswomen's Guilds

Women's Holiday Centre
The Women's Directory – Galley 49
Women's League of Health and
   Beauty
Women's Sports Foundation (WSF)
See also Holidays; Social/cultural
   activities; Sports/exercise

REFLEXOLOGY

Women's Natural Health Centre

REFUGES

Chiswick Family Rescue
Women's Aid Federation (England)

RELAXATION

Vineyard Project

RELIGIOUS ORGANISATIONS

Baha'i National Women's Committee
Women in Theology
See also Catholic church
   organisations; Christian
   organisations; Jewish organisations

RESEARCH

*Many of the organisations listed in the
directory carry out research as part
of their work.*
Birthright
Centre for Women's Studies
Child Poverty Action Group
CREW
Low Pay Unit
National Osteoporosis Society
One Plus One (Marriage and
   Partnership Research)
PROGRESS (Campaign for Research
   into Human Reproduction)

RESOURCE CENTRES/
LIBRARIES

Christian Women's Information and
   Resources (CWIRES)
Fawcett Library
Feminist Archive
Feminist Audio Books (FAB)
Feminist Library

Lesbian Archive and Information
   Centre (LAIC)
London Lesbian and Gay Centre
Midwives Information and Resource
   Service (MIDIRS)
Multiple Births Foundation
National Organisation for Women's
   Management Education (NOWME)
One Plus One (Marriage and
   Partnership Research)
Pankhurst Trust
Peace House
Practical Alternatives for Mums, Dads
   and Under-Fives (PRAM)
Women Artist's Slide Library
Women's Health and Reproductive
   Rights Information Centre
Women's Media Resource Project
Women's Resource Centre
See also Advice and information
   services

RESPITE CARE

Break
See also Holidays

RETT SYNDROME

National Rett Syndrome Association
   (NRSA)

RETURN TO WORK

Centre for Women's Studies
Industrial Society, Pepperell Unit
Milton Keynes Women and Work
   Group
National Housewives Association
   (NHA)
Women in Training
Women Returners' Network

RIGHTS

See Employment rights; Human rights;
   Law and justice; Patient's rights;
   Welfare rights; Women's rights

RUBELLA (GERMAN MEASLES)

National Rubella Council

SAFETY
See Environmental health; Personal safety

SCIENCE
Open University Women into Science and Engineering (WISE) Group

SELF HELP
Agoraphobia Information Service
Al-Anon Family Groups
Alcoholics Anonymous (AA)
Asian Young Women's Project (AYWP)
Beaumont Society
Brittle Bone Society
Eating Disorders Association
Endometriosis Society
Gender Dysphoria Trust (GDT)
Gingerbread
Hysterectomy Support Group (HSG)
Lifeline – Help for Victims of Violence in the Home
London Black Women's Health Action Project
Meet-a-Mum Association (MAMA)
Money Management Council
NAPS National Headquarters (National Association for Premenstrual Syndrome)
National Federation of Self-Help Organisations
National Information for Parents of Prematures: Education, Resources and Support (NIPPERS)
National Self-Help Support Networks
Network for Supporing Children of People with Mental Distress (NSCPMD)
Northern Concord
Overeaters Anonymous
Parent Network
Spare Tyre
StepfamilY
Steroid Action Group
Twins and Multiple Births Association
Working Mothers Association

SEPARATION
See Divorce and separation

SEXUAL ABUSE
See Child abuse; Domestic violence; Incest; Rape; Sexual harassment

SEX DISCRIMINATION/SEXISM/ SEX EQUALITY
Black Women for Wages for Housework
Campaign Against Pornography and Censorship (CPC)
Fawcett Society
Letterbox Library
National Association of Local Government Women's Committees
Sex, Race, Class (Black and Third World Women's Discussion and Study Group) (SRC)
Time Off for Women
Trades Union Congress
Women Against Sexual Harassment (WASH)
Women, Heritage and Museums
Women in Education: The National Association
Women's Legal Defence Fund
Women's Resource Centre
See also Equal opportunities

SEXUAL HARASSMENT
Trades Union Congress
Woman Against Rape
Women Against Sexual Harassment (WASH)
Woman's Aid Federation (England)

SEXUAL HEALTH
Brook Advisory Centres
Family Planning Association
Institute for the Study of Christianity and Sexuality
Marie Stopes House

SEXUAL IDENTITY
Beaumont Society
Gender Dysphoria Trust (GDT)

Identity
London Friend
London Lesbian Line (LLL)
Northern Concord
Partners Group for Partners and
 Families of Transexuals
See also Gays/lesbians;
 Transvestites/transsexuals

SEXUAL PROBLEMS

Brook Advisory Centres
Relate (National Marriage Guidance)
SPOD (Association to Aid the Sexual
 and Personal Relationships of
 People with a Disability)
See also Gays/lesbians; Marriage
 counselling; Sexual identity;
 Transvestites/transsexuals

SHOPLIFTING

Crisis Counselling for Alleged
 Shoplifters
Portia Trust

SINGLE PARENTS

See One-parent families

SOCIAL/CULTURAL ACTIVITIES

Asian Young Women's Project
 (AYWP)
Bangladesh Women's Association in
 Great Britain
British Federation of University
 Women
Brothers and Sisters Club
Farm Women's Club
Gemma
Gingerbread
Girl Guides Association
International Catholic Society for Girls
 (ACISJF)
Kenric
Lesbian and Gay Pride Organising
 Committee
Lesbian and Gay Youth Movement
 (LGYM)
London Lesbian and Gay Centre
Mature Lesbian Group
Meet-a-Mum Association (MAMA)
National Association of Ladies'
 Circles of Great Britain and Ireland
National Association of Widows
National Council for the Divorced and
 Separated
National Federation of Women's
 Institutes (NFWI)
National Women's Register
Pascal Theatre Company
Sangam Association for Asian
 Women
Townswomen's Guilds
Union of Turkish Women in Britain
 (UTWB)
West Indian Women's Association
Women, Heritage and Museums
Young Women's Christian Association
 of Great Britain (YWCA)
See also Arts; Cultural links between
 countries

SOCIAL SECURITY

See Welfare rights/benefits

SOCIALISM

European Forum of Socialist
 Feminists – UK Group

SPORTS/EXERCISE

Women's League of Health and
 Beauty
Women's Sports Foundation (WSF)
See also Recreation/leisure

STATUS OF WOMEN

See Position of women in society

STEPFAMILIES

Stepfamily

STERILISATION

Birth Control Campaign
Birth Control Trust
British Pregnancy Advisory Service
Marie Stopes House
Pregnancy Advisory Service
See also Birth control

STEROIDS
Steroid Aid Group

STRESS
Industrial Society, Pepperell Unit
Parents Anonymous (London)
Suzy Lamplugh Trust
Vineyard Project

'TALKING BOOKS'
Feminist Audio Books (FAB)
Women's Tapeover

TOXOPLASMOSIS
Toxoplasmosis Trust

TRADES UNIONS
Royal College of Nursing
Trades Union Congress

TRAINING
See Education and Training

TRANQUILISER OVERUSE
Vineyard Project

TRANSLATION
See Interpretation and translation

TRANSPORT
Women for Improved Transport (WIT)

TRANSVESTITES/ TRANSSEXUALS
Beaumont Society
Gender Dysphoria Trust (GDT)
Northern Concord
Partners Group for Partners and Families of Transexuals
Transvestite/Transsexual Support Group (TV/TS Group)

TWINS/MULTIPLE BIRTHS
Multiple Births Foundation
Twins and Multiple Births Association

TURKS
Union of Turkish Women in Britain (UTWB)

UMBRELLA OGANISATIONS
See Co-ordinating/umbrella bodies

VDUs (VISUAL DISPLAY UNITS)
City Centre
VDU Workers' Rights Campaign
See also Computers

VICTIMS OF CRIME
Rape Crisis Centre
Victims' Helpline
Women Against Rape

VIOLENCE
See Child abuse; Domestic violence; Rape; Victims of crime

VOLUNTEERING/COMMUNITY SERVICE
Catholic Women's League
Co-operative Women's Guild
Girl Guides Association
Girls Venture Corps Aid Cadets
National Association of Ladies' Circles of Great Britain and Ireland
National Free Church Women's Council
Soroptimist International of Great Britain and Ireland
Women's Royal Voluntary Service

WAGES FOR HOUSEWORK
Black Women for Wages for Housework
Time Off for Women
Wages Due Lesbians
Wages for Housework Campaign

WEIGHT PROBLEMS
Feed-Back
Overeaters Anonymous
Spare Tyre
See also Anorexia/bulimia nervosa

WELFARE RIGHTS/BENEFITS

Bangladesh Women's Association in Great Britain
Child Poverty Action Group
Cypriot Women's League
FAEERU (Women's Group)
Low Pay Unit
Maternity Alliance
Maternity Services Liaison Committee
National Association of Citizens Advice Bureaux (NACAB)
National Council for the Divorced and Separated
National Council for One-Parent Families
Sangam Association for Asian Women
War Widows' Association of Great Britain
West Indian Women's Association
See also Poverty: UK

WIDOWS

National Association of Widows
War Widows' Association of Great Britain

WOMEN DOCTORS

Medical Women's Federation

WOMEN: HEALTH

Active Birth Centre
Anorexics Anonymous
Associated Country Women of the World
Association for Improvements in the Maternity Services (AIMS)
Association for Post-Natal Illness
Birthright
Breast Cancer Research Trust
Breast Cancer and Mastectomy Association
British Pregnancy Advisory Service
Brittle Bone Society
Caesarian Support Group of Cambridge
Cervical Stitch Network
Child
City Centre
Copper 7 Association
Cystitis and Candida
Dalkon Shield Association
Elizabeth Garrett Anderson Action Committee
Endometriosis Society
Family Planning Association
Feed-Back
Foundation for Women's Health, Research and Development (FORWARD)
Genetic Clinic
Health Rights
Helene Harris Memorial Trust
Hysterectomy Support Group (HSG)
London Black Women's Health Action Project
Marie Stopes House
Maternity Alliance
Maternity Links
Maternity Services Liason Scheme
Miscarriage Association
NAPS National Headquarters (National Association for Premenstrual Syndrome)
National Abortion Campaign
National Association for the Childless
National Osteoporosis Society
National Rett Syndrome Association
Positively Women
Premenstrual Society (PREMSOC)
SARA (Society for the Advancement of Research into Anorexia)
Spare Tyre
Steroid Action Group
Women's Health and Reproductive Rights Information Centre
Women's Health Concern (WHC)
Women's Health Information and Support Centre
Women's Health Network
Women's National Cancer Control Campaign
Women's Natural Health Centre
Women's Nutritional Advisory Service
Women's Therapy Centre
See also Birth control; Menopause; Pregnancy/childbirth; Premenstrual syndrome/tension

WOMEN'S HISTORY

See History

WOMEN'S RIGHTS

Afro-Caribbean Educational Project Women's Group
Cypriot Women's League
English Collective of Prostitutes (ECP)
Fawcett Library
King's Cross Women's Centre
Latin American Women's Rights Service
National Alliance of Women's Organisations
National Assembly of Women
National Network for International Solidarity
Rights of Women
Singapore and Malaysian British Association (SIMBA) Women's Section)
WinVisible (Women with Visible and Invisible Disabilities)
Women's Centre (Northern Ireland Women's Rights Movement

WOMEN'S STUDIES

Centre for Women's Studies
Fawcett Library
Sex, Race and Class (Black and Third World Women's Discussion and Study Group) (SRC)

WORKING WOMEN

National Joint Committee of Working Women's Organisations
New Ways to Work
Over Forty Association for Women Workers
Women Returners' Network
Women Working Worldwide
Working Mothers Association
Working for Childcare/Workplace Nurseries
See also Careers; Employment; Employment rights

WRITING/PUBLISHING

Everywoman Publishing Ltd
Feminist Library
Gay Authors Workshop
Letterbox Library
Women in Publishing

YOUNG PEOPLE

Asian Young Women's Project (AYWP)
Girl Guides Association
Girls Alone Project
Girls' Brigade
Girls Friendly Society and Townsend Fellowship
Girls' Public School Day Trust
Girls' Schools Association
International Catholic Society for Girls (ACISJF)
Lesbian and Gay Youth Movement (LGYM)
Scout and Guide Graduate Association (SAGGA)
Streetwise Youth Project
Trust for the Study of Adolescence
Young Women's Christian Association of Great Britain (YWCA)

BSP Directories

The Voluntary Agencies Directory

The Social Activists' Bible

NCVO's directory of voluntary agencies is the standard reference work for anyone who cares about helping the community. It lists nearly 2,000 leading voluntary agencies, ranging from small, specialist self-help groups to long-established national charities. It gives concise, up-to-date descriptions of their aims and activities, with details of

- charitable status
- volunteer participation
- trading activities
- local branches
- membership
- staffing

A list of useful addresses includes professional and public advisory bodies concerned with voluntary action; a classified index and quick reference list of acronyms and abbreviations give easy access to entries.

There is extensive coverage of new groups concerned with women's issues, minority rights, self help, community development and leisure activities, environment and conservation, campaigning and consumer affairs.

Voluntary agencies play an important part in making the world a better place to live in. This NCVO directory is the essential guide to their work.

'If you buy only one directory of voluntary agencies, buy this one and buy it every year.' *Health Libraries Review*

'an essential working tool' *Environment Now*

The Parents' Directory
Compiled by Fiona Macdonald
Foreword by Esther Rantzen

'Whatever the problem . . . you only need spend a few minutes glancing through the pages of *The Parents' Directory* to see what an astonishing variety of voluntary bodies there are for parents to turn to . . . an excellent and comprehensive map.'
Esther Rantzen

The Parents' Directory lists around 800 voluntary organisations which are able to give help, advice and information to parents on a wide range of topics. The information is presented in easily accessible form under the headings Education, Family Welfare, Handicap, Health and Leisure, with each entry giving details of aims and objects, contact names, addresses and telephone numbers. Symbols are used to give additional information in the same manner as that outlined for *The Health Directory*.

The Women's Directory
Compiled by Fiona Macdonald

The Women's Directory will enable women who wish to make contact with others – whether for social, cultural, sporting, charitable, self-help or political purposes – to locate and identify suitable groups and organisations. It refers women to appropriate 'umbrella' bodies, whether voluntary, local-government-based or state funded, and gives other sources of information about women's activities, including relevant magazines and journals, publishers and bookshops. Presented in an accessible, simple-to-follow format, with symbols used to give additional information in the same manner as that outlined for *The Health Directory*.

In addition to this book and other titles listed, **Bedford Square Press** publishes books on a range of current social issues. Series published include Survival Handbooks, Community Action, Practical Guides, Society Today, Directories, Reports, Organisation and Management, and Fundraising.

If you would like to receive a copy of the current catalogue, or further details of any title listed in this book, please complete the coupon below and forward it to:

> Sales Department
> Bedford Square Press
> NCVO
> 26 Bedford Square
> London WC1B 3HU
>
> Tel: 071-636 4066 (x2212)

☐   Please send me your latest catalogue/booklist (please tick)

☐   Please send me further details of the following titles:

> 1. _____
>
> 2. _____
>
> 3. _____
>
> 4. _____

☐   Please add my name to your regular mailing list. My areas of interest are (please state):

_____

NAME: _____

ADDRESS: _____

_____

_____Post code: _____

(You may photocopy this page).